TECHNICAL VIRGINS

TECHNICAL VIRGINS

Elaine Crowley

THE LILLIPUT PRESS

First published 1998 by
THE LILLIPUT PRESS LTD
62-63 Sitric Road, Arbour Hill,
Dublin 7, Ireland.

A CIP record for this
title is available from
The British Library.

ISBN 1 901866 23 8

The Lilliput Press receives financial assistance from
An Chomhairle Ealaíon/The Arts Council of Ireland.

Set in 10 on 12 Galliard by Sheila Stephenson
Printed in Ireland by Betaprint of Clonshaugh, Dublin

PROLOGUE

The train, as if impatient to start its journey north, huffed and puffed its plume of smoke towards the station's glass-panelled roof. The June sun shone onto the waiting passengers; onto the beady-eyed waddling pigeons searching for anything edible. The sun added to the discomfort of the men loading the guards' van with sacks of mail, boxes, crates, packages and parcels.

Sweat beaded on the faces of the porters carrying heavy expensive luggage towards first-class carriages. Young boys, dirty, unkempt, mitching from school, some barefoot, some wearing boots several sizes too big, touted less prosperous passengers. 'D'ye want your case carried, mister?' they asked, wiping faces and noses with torn sleeves of their shirts and gansies. Giving the 'ride on that till you get a pony' salute to railway employees who threatened to kick their arses if they didn't get to Hell's Gates out of their way.

Around the station kiosk people pushed and shoved their way to the counter, bought newspapers and asked hopefully if there were any cigarettes. 'Are you coddin' me?' the assistant replied. 'Sure for all the cigarettes that are about, the war might still be on.'

Not far from the kiosk a group of young girls in ill-assorted outfits stood close together. They wore faded summer frocks, too long or too short. Some had topped the frocks with costume jackets in serge, flannel and tweed; all the garments gave the appearance of having had a previous owner …

The girls were mostly pretty. Good complexions. Dark-haired and fair. Ginger and auburn. Straight hair combed up into sweeps secured with clips, frizzy perms; and one girl with long straight blonde hair wore it in the style of Veronica Lake.

Now and then with a toss of her head shaking it back to look up at the station clock. Around their feet were shabby cardboard suitcases secured with belts or pieces of rope. They talked loudly, laughed and giggled nervously. One, after glancing up at the station clock, began to cry. Her companions offered her words of comfort, cigarettes from paper packets of Woodbines. Green packets decorated with honeysuckle. 'Have a bull's eye,' one suggested and, with difficulty, prised from the depths of a newspaper cone a sticky hard-boiled black and white sweet. 'Go on,' she urged, 'take it.' The girl sniffed and sobbed, then wiped her eyes, took a sweet and began to suck.

A little apart from the group two other girls and a woman stood. The woman wore a black edge-to-edge coat over a dusky pink dress and a black straw hat tilted becomingly over one eye. Her shoes were suede, high-heeled and in good condition. To the older of the two girls she talked earnestly. From time to time the girl nodded as if agreeing with what was being said. Expressions of irritation and embarrassment flitted across the younger girl's face.

The guard's van closed. Passengers who had loitered now began to board the train. The woman threw her arms around the younger girl, held her close and kissed her. A railway employee walked along the platform slamming doors. The group picked up their suitcases and moved forward. One called to the others, 'We'll squash into the same carriage.' The girl disengaged herself from her mother and followed them. At the end of the train a man waved a green flag. The train began its journey to Belfast.

TECHNICAL VIRGINS

ONE

In four days I had learned to answer to Paddy, Cock, Chuck, Kid and, occasionally, Cloth-Ears. To dress and undress before twenty-three strangers. To make my bed on biscuits: to unmake and barrack it. To sleep in a room almost devoid of furniture, curtainless and cheerless. To eat for breakfast steamed fish, grey in colour, surrounded on the plate by equally grey water; leathery sausages with tasteless insides; reconstituted eggs that were pallid and, whether served scrambled or as omelettes, flavourless and rubbery; to drink hot, sweet tea brewed in urns as big as a washday boiler. Tea rumoured to be strengthened with washing soda and spiked with bromide to dull our sexual urges.

I had left my home in Dublin, gone to Belfast and from there sailed across the Irish Sea in a force-nine gale, transferred to a packed train, suffocated almost by smoke and smuts, then ridden in the back of an army vehicle to my eventual destination, an army barracks in a Cheshire town, to be trained as a woman soldier.

In Belfast I took the King's shilling, signed on for two years and became a member of the Women's Auxiliary Territorial Service. All this I did for love. Not for King and country but for the love of a man. A man I adored with all the love of my seventeen-year-old heart … my first and only love, who could send shivers up my spine, make me feel faint, blush, tremble, lose my appetite and light candles to the patron saint of hopeless causes. For if ever there was a hopeless cause my love affair was one.

The object of my passion, hopes and dejection wasn't aware of my existence. I loved from across the street, from glimpses in the chip shop, across aisles in mass. I watched him in the dance-halls tangoing, foxtrotting in the arms of glamorous dancers.

7

I walked miles around the city hoping for a sight of him. I found where he lived and haunted the street. And on occasions when I saw him I pretended great interest in the nearest shop window. Through it I saw how tall he was. How well built. His trench coat and soft hat … Like Humphrey Bogart, only handsomer. Humphrey Bogart had an ugly face. My love looked like Victor Mature. I'd seen the flash of his white teeth, his big brown eyes.

In work I talked about him to anyone who would listen. I dreamt about him, wakening just as he was about to kiss me and declare his love. Closed my eyes and tried to sleep again, to recapture the dream. My mother said she thought I was run down. I might need a tonic. Or maybe I was costive. There followed an inquisition about my bowels. She promised a dose of opening medicine.

Sometimes, often, studying myself in the mirror I saw the reason why I didn't attract him. I was tall for my age, lumpy, my nose was too long, my eyes too small, my hair lank brown, straight and cut as if a pudding basin had covered it while the shearing took place. And my breasts bobbed inside my jumpers. My mother promised to buy me a brassière. But like many of her promises it never materialized.

And then one day in a magazine the solution stared me in the face. I would go to England. Join the ATS. I was looking at a recruiting advertisement for the Women's Service. Looking at the girl in her uniform. Tall and elegant, sleek blonde hair crowned by a perky little cap, wearing an expertly cut tunic in fine barathea the colour of sand with the sun on it.

I would join up. The uniform would transform me. I'd come back to Dublin wearing it. I would meet him in my uniform the colour of pale golden sand. He would notice me for the first time. He wouldn't be able to resist me. How could he? How could any man resist the look-alike girl in the recruiting poster?

My mind was made up. Nothing would be allowed to stand in my way. But because I wasn't eighteen, I needed my mother's consent to join the forces. She reared up when I asked for it. 'Go to England, that den of iniquity, well indeed you won't put the fur of your foot near it. Women are being raped and murdered every day of the week over there. Given drugged drinks and cigarettes and sold into the white slave traffic. And that's apart from the bombs showering down on them blowing them to smithereens. What put that idea into your head?'

She wouldn't understand or sympathize with unrequited love. So I pleaded lack of job satisfaction. 'I hate tailoring. I'm fed up day in day out machining sleeve linings.'

'Who likes their work?' she retorted. 'You think of no one but yourself ... I moved out of the scheme after your daddy died to make life easier for you. We're back in the street. I'm just getting back on my feet and you want to clear off ... Well you're not and that's that.'

I pleaded and coaxed, ranted and raved. She countered all my tactics with gruesome accounts of atrocities committed in England. Charles Peace, Burke and Hare, Buck Ruxton, and when the list of ordinary murderers ran out, there was Henry VIII, his daughter Elizabeth, and Cromwell.

'Prostitutes, whoremasters, murderers and pagans the lot of them, you're not going and that's that.'

'My daddy was English.'

'The Lord have mercy on him, his mother was Irish and a Catholic.'

'And in any case in two months I'll be eighteen and won't need your letter,' I said when she stopped for breath. For a moment she was at a loss for words. But only for a moment. Then back she came, 'You always were a self-willed little bitch. I haven't forgotten when you bought a coat unknownst to me.' My beautiful heliotrope-coloured coat. We seldom had a row without her reminding me of the deception I had practised to get it. 'No thought for anyone but yourself,' she continued, smoothing a brown paper bag. She smoothed and saved brown paper bags and bits of string. 'How am I going to manage without your £1 a week coming in, answer me that?'

'You're a widow. You'll get a dependant's allowance. It says so in the forms.' I'd slipped up.

She pounced. 'What forms?' Her eyes bored into me. Before their gimlet gaze I couldn't lie.

'I sent for them. It's all there about the allowance in black and white.' Black and white was a favourite phrase of hers. She had great faith in the written word.

Putting on her Woolworth's glasses many times reinforced with wire, she took the forms I produced. 'They write in double-Dutch,' she said as she perused the paragraph dealing with allowances. Her lips formed each word silently as she read.

9

I watched her, filled with elation as I did so. I was free. I was escaping. Then suddenly I was deflated. What was I doing? What was I letting myself in for? Why was I leaving home?

To escape from her, I told myself. No more rows, no more nagging. Come and go as I pleased. Make new friends, see new places.

Her lips were still working over the letter's official jargon. She appeared to have shrunk. She looked like an old woman. Seeing her like that, I remembered the day after my father's funeral when I came home from work and she was sitting by the fire, huddled and dejected, fingering the pound notes spread on the table.

'Every undertaker's yard in the city collected for your daddy. He was very well liked. Lord have mercy on him—the comfort I could have given him with half of that. D'ye know what I was doing when you came in?'

'No.'

'I was just thinking—I have everything. Everything I ever wanted. A house and all that money. Everything I ever wished for. Everything—and I've nothing for I haven't got him.'

That day three years ago I sat and cried with her. Not for long. She never cried for long, and in any case there was my dinner to dish up. Instead she reminisced about when she'd first met my father. The handsomest, smartest soldier in the British Army, and after the Treaty, when he transferred to the Free State Army, the smartest one in that.

'People,' she said as she teemed the potatoes into the slop bucket, 'used to stop to look after him in the street.' She put the pot back over a low flame and continued talking, shaking the pot as she did so. 'They're nice and dry now. What was I saying? Ah, yes, about how smart he was. He was a great horseman as well. Could ride from when he was child, his grandfather in Horsham kept horses.

'Sometimes, in between jobs in the undertakers, he'd get work in the riding school up in the Park. Bridie in the Iveagh Market used to keep the breeches and leggings for me. He liked to knock about with the horsy crowd in Queen Street. D'ye remember him in the breeches and leggings?'

'Yes,' I said, my voice choked with tears I was trying to repress. Choked with sadness and the guilt of a memory from a few years before he died. I must have been about eleven then. I was coming out of school as the 83 bus stopped at the terminus on Cashel Road. And my father stepped down from the platform. He was drunk and I tried to avoid him spotting me. But he did and whistled his melodious whistle to attract my attention.

He was staggering slightly, his bowler hat pushed to the back of his head. I prayed silently for the ground to open and swallow him up before any of my pals would see him. It didn't and he came to me and embraced me. Asked, as he always did, how I had got on in school. Had a treat in his pocket for me—a penny bar of chocolate.

'What has you in bad humour—that's not like you,' he said, taking my hand in his. I mumbled an excuse and we walked on, me imagining everyone from school watching us and nudging each other. 'Look at her oul' fella, mouldy drunk,' they'd be saying. During the walk home, for the first time in my life, I hated and was ashamed of him. But at the same time I would have scrawbed the face off anyone who dared to pass a remark on him.

The dinner was ready. I sat to the table for it, and only referred to remembering well my father in his riding breeches. Putting the lamb chop on top of the cabbage so the meat juices would flavour it, my mother said, 'God help him, he worked for six years dying on his feet. His chest, you know, it was always delicate.'

Even after having seen his death certificate and numerous doctors confirming the diagnosis of tuberculosis, she would never admit that's what he had. She continued to reminisce. 'Months before he died he volunteered to go into Our Lady's Hospice for the Dying. He did that,' she said, 'for our sake. So the bit of food would go further and his cough wouldn't disturb us during the night.'

Then her memory switched to happier times. She and I recalled him dancing a jig, tapping out tunes on the oven door and asking us to guess what they were. Planting his garden. Robbing the granite doorstep from the building site and with superhuman strength lifting it onto the baby's go-car, getting it back to the house, up the steps, and into the back garden. It was to have been used to make a rockery. But his strength was used up then and forever. The granite could not be broken. The step remained where it had been dumped and was used as a seat.

My mother's moods changed like quicksilver. Suddenly the pleasant reminiscences were done with. 'D'ye know,' she said, 'you're a bloody little bitch. I searched high and low for my scissors all day and couldn't find it. Where did you put it?'

She would go on for hours like this if I didn't produce the scissors. Which I couldn't. And now there was no daddy to either defuse or deflect her. These were the times when I missed him so much.

I was only fifteen. Life outside the house beckoned me. I promised I'd search for the scissors when I came back but first I had to call to a friend's house. I wouldn't be a minute.

'Have a cup of tea before you go,' she said. There was neither spite nor vengeance in her nature. I was never what is now called grounded, never confined to my bedroom, never deprived of food. All only talk, talk, and idle threats to kill, cut the legs from under you or break your neck.

When I came back she was as likely to be telling or reading my sister a story, having a row with my brother, or one of her women friends might be there consoling and crying with her, or giving out yards about the next-door neighbour.

That's how our life was. The three years since my father's death didn't alter it. He was missed and cried over, laughed over and never for a day completely forgotten. It was a house of warmth and forgiveness. A house of love and safety. A house where although you might consider yourself grown up my mother would still lash out with her hand. And later in the night when you were just falling asleep, she'd tiptoe into your room, adjust the bedcovers and sprinkle you with Holy Water while she murmured prayers to bring you safely through the night. More often than not the water fell on your face and woke you up.

And here I was about to leave it all. The abiding love, the security. A mother who was always there for you. Who'd stick up for you. ('My child', as she said about each of us in turn, 'wouldn't do such a thing.' But if you were in the wrong you'd be chastised.) Who above all was so forgiving. Who forgave my father when he confessed he had been unfaithful to her. Who tracked down his paramour and put an end to their affair. And forgave him when he beat her up for doing so.

My mother who was the cranky, joyous spirit of our home and hearts. Who nursed my father until he went into the hospice. Who walked there in hail, rain and snow, the piece of cardboard covering the hole in the sole of her shoe sodden and squelching. Who had three children as volatile and as strong-willed as she was, who fought her every inch of the way when her mood was quarrelsome—though looking back now I suppose it was the response she wanted.

How could I leave all this? Go amongst strangers? Enter a world I knew nothing about? Who would slip a hot jar beside my feet when they were cold? Draw a boil to a head with the heated neck of a bottle? Make me thin gruel with a teaspoon of whiskey in it when I had a cold? Make me a 'guggie in a cup' if I was off my food?

These memories and thoughts chased each other through my mind as she finished the letter. She took off her glasses, put them in the pocket of her pinny and the letter on the mantelpiece. While doing so she noticed the time. 'God!' she exclaimed, 'it's after six, if I don't hurry I'll miss the paperman and I'm follying up that murder trial.'

She had her coat on and was out the door in a flash. I heard the front door slam and life beckoned to me again. My mother would be all right. I'd be all right. We were survivors.

I got the letter of consent and went to Belfast for an interview and medical examination. On the train I met several girls also hoping to join up. In the barracks to which we reported I saw khaki uniforms for the first time. They looked nothing like the one in the recruiting poster. The colour wasn't a goldy sand colour. More like the dictionary definition, which I had looked up: 'Of Persian or Urdu origin, meaning dusty.' These uniforms were drab and dusty, but I consoled myself that it was age and long wear. Mine, the one in which I'd cause a sensation in Dublin and captivate my love, would be dazzlingly new.

* * *

'Childhood illnesses?' the medical officer asked. I listed them, my heart thundering with fear as I anticipated his next question and the lies I must tell.

'Parents living?'

'My father's dead.'

'What did he die of?'

'An accident, sir, he was knocked down and killed.'

My mother had tutored me well. Never, never, and especially

13

to a doctor, did you admit that there was tuberculosis in your family. There was a stigma attached to the disease. You were often shunned, as AIDS sufferers are today. As a relative of the infected person you felt the guilt and shame. Euphemisms were used. A touch delicate, asthma, a weakness left over from a childhood pneumonia or pleurisy. Employers sometimes refused you work. Parents came between courting couples.

During the seven years my father had the disease my mother admitted to no one, not even herself, that tuberculosis was what ailed him. All his X-rays, positive sputum tests, weight loss, fever-flushed cheeks, night sweats and racking cough didn't convince her. Not even his death certificate, on which the cause of death was given as phthisis. 'Look,' she said, pointing to the Latin word of Greek origin for a wasting disease, especially tuberculosis. 'Wasn't I right all along? I knew he never had consumption. That's what killed him,' she said pointing to the unpronounceable word. 'That little cur in the Meath Hospital didn't know his arse from his elbow. Probably out of the College of Surgeons.'

She had tutored me well. Blatantly I lied to the medical officer, elaborating on the accident that killed my father. For she had warned me, 'Once you admit to a doctor about consumption they'd start prying and probing. Sending you to clinics for more probing and X-rays. Shadows, patches, things that you were unaware of and didn't interfere with you might be discovered. Then you were in their hands. Your body never your own again.'

My lie was accepted, my heart, lungs and liver declared sound. I was passed A1 and given a date on which to return and sign away my freedom. And so, on 17 June 1945, I arrived at the camp in Cheshire.

The people in the tailoring factory made a collection. Thirty shillings, I think. More money than I had ever owned before. From it I bought my first deodorant. A push-up stick of O-Do-Rono. The owning and using of it made me feel grown-up and sophisticated. I had presents from relations. A short-sleeved, maroon, hand-knitted jumper, a rosary and a prayer book. A change of clothes, still minus a brassière, and my beautiful coat. Cream and green tweed, made to measure with a dark-green velvet collar. There were always tailors in the trade who did 'nicksers', using the firm's time and often their trimmings as

well. That's how I came by the coat. Apart from those possessions, the only other items I owned were toothpaste, a tooth-
brush and a comb.

My mother came to see me off. She looked very smart in her
edge-to-edge coat. After sizing up a group of girls who were
travelling with me to Belfast she singled one out from the
crowd. A Dublin girl whose name was Deirdre, stout, rosy-
cheeked and, in my opinion, years older than me. My mother
talked in a voice she used in public, especially in the presence of
men, laughing her lovely laugh. Now and then looking round
to see if anyone was paying her attention.

I was mortified and prayed for the train to leave soon. When
it did she followed it along the platform, still talking, advising,
waving, dabbing at her tears with a dainty handkerchief. I, too,
leant out of the window waving until the train turned a bend
and, to my great relief, took me out of her sight.

TWO

Lt was the effect of the injections against smallpox and varieties of typhoid fever: I hadn't recovered from the journey. I was disorientated from the confusing experiences since I'd arrived in the camp, punch-drunk with the slang and army jargon. Biscuits were three-piece mattresses; barracking was a way of sandwiching your sheets between two blankets then wrapping the lot in a third, so that the bundle resembled a monster brown-and-white Liquorice Allsort. Rookies and jankers, fizzers and bulling, knickers called wrist-stranglers. My mind was unhinged. I was hallucinating. For why else, everywhere I looked, did I see pairs of naked breasts? High round ones, slack pendulous ones, pert tip-tilted, minute to the point of non-existence. It wasn't modest to look on another's nakedness. According to my Catholic rearing it wasn't modest to look on one's own. And not having a full-length glass at home, I never had.

I looked away. I shook my head to clear it. I had a fever, that was it. I was delirious. I looked back again and the breasts were still there and naked women splashing water at each other, laughing and singing, 'In a strange caravan there's a lady they call the gypsy.' And then I saw the strangest sight of all. A pair of widely spaced breasts and growing in the space between a bunch of curly ginger hair. Banging her chest, the owner of the breasts began doing Tarzan imitations, then yelled, 'What d'ye think of the running water, Pad?' her voice rising above the singers. 'Eh, Cloth-Ears, it's you I'm talking to.'

'Me?' I shouted back.

'Yeah, you, Chuck. What d'ye think of the running water, great isn't it?'

My head cleared. I wasn't feverish nor having hallucinations. We were having a communal shower, something I'd never experienced before. And I was Cloth-Ears, Pad and Chuck. The wide-spaced breasts and chest hair were Edith's … also a new recruit, a rookie, but the daughter of an old soldier who showed us the ropes. Covering my nakedness with an army-issue towel ('for the use of', a phrase I didn't, and never did, understand) I stepped onto a duckboard and called to Edith, 'The water's great.' I had answered in the same vein to questions as to how I found wearing shoes, what I thought of electricity, flush lavatories, buses and trains. Recognizing from the good-humoured voices asking the questions that malice was not intended.

'You're alright, Pad,' Edith assured me while pulling on her khaki knickers with well-elasticated legs. 'Pity the bugger who tries to get his hand up these,' she laughed and, braless, went to a shelf where she had left her cigarettes. 'Want a fag, kid?' she asked, proffering a packet of Park Drive.

'Ta,' I said, using the word for the first time in my life.

* * *

For four days we had been confined to barracks. During this time our uniforms were issued, and injections and vaccines given. We spent the days nursing sore arms and marking kits with our names and numbers, meeting Corporal Robinson, our squad leader, and getting to know each other.

Twenty-four girls occupied the barrack room. Half were from Cheshire and Lancashire, the other half those who had travelled from Dublin with me.

On the way back from the communal shower Edith reminded us that tomorrow for the first time we would wear uniforms. 'We'll get started on the bulling after tea.'

Already I had taken a great liking to Edith and her friend Marjorie. They came from the same seaside town and had been friends all their lives. They were both low-sized, stocky; they resembled each other except that Edith's hair was ginger and curly like the hair on her chest, and Marj's blonde with dark roots and permed. They were good-natured and funny. I found it difficult to understand their dialect but was learning. I would have liked to ditch Deirdre, my minder, but wherever I went she was close behind.

After dinner we could unbarrack our beds, lie or sit on them, or get under the covers and sleep. Anything we liked, provided no one else shared the bed. This had been stressed at a lecture on the day after we arrived at barracks. 'It's an offence for which you can be charged,' the officer informed us.

Afterwards Edith answered our questions as to why you could be charged. 'You know how some fellas'd do a frog if it stopped hopping? According to my Dad there's girls like that too.' We gasped in disbelief. Fellas maybe, but girls? Then one of the Irish girls said, 'I'll tell you one thing, no one will lie on mine. All my life I slept two or three to a bed. Sometimes four. Two at the top and two at the foot. It was nothing to wake up with my granny's big toe nearly poking my eye out. Separate beds are gorgeous, so they are.' The majority of us, having been reared in the same circumstance, agreed with her.

We lounged on our beds, we smoked and talked, and I, eager to familiarize myself with army slang, quizzed Edith. 'A charge', she explained, 'is the same as a fizzer.'

'Why d'ye get put on a fizzer?'

'All sorts of things. Being late on parade, not barracking your bed properly, insubordination, talking back, coming in after roll call, belting an NCO or officer, millions of things. She recited a long, long list of offences which carried sentences that varied from forty-eight hours confined to barracks, to jankers, which she explained might be cleaning rooms, bumpering floors or kitchen fatigues. 'That's peeling sacks and sacks of spuds.'

Edith now had a captive audience and continued. 'For some things you could have your pay stopped or even finish up in the glasshouse.'

Marj contradicted her, 'Hang on, cock, you're talking about soldiers. Women don't get sent to the glasshouse.'

'Maybe I'm wrong about that,' Edith conceded, 'but not about nothing else.'

Bubbles, the only girl in the squad who owned a dressing-gown and spoke like the BBC newsreader and Corporal Robinson, and whom Edith had nicknamed because her hair was like the picture advertising Pears' soap of a boy blowing bubbles, asked Edith, 'What is the glasshouse?'

'Military prison. Terrible place. No food, only bread and water. Get flogged if you look crooked, so my Dad says.'

'Sounds like something out of Dickens,' Bubbles said in a voice that cast disbelief on Edith's statement.

'Clever clogs. If you don't believe me don't ask questions in future.'

'Sorry,' said Bubbles, who didn't seem sorry at all. She adroitly changed the subject and talked about the following day, how we'd fare during our first session of square-bashing, which Edith had informed us was slang for drilling on the square.

'I'm petrified just thinking about it,' Deirdre said. 'I hope there'll be no fellas watching us.' According to her she was so shy and retiring that almost everything terrified her. But not, I said to myself, strange fellas on boats. And while the girls discussed the pros and cons of drilling on the square my mind went back to the night we had crossed from Belfast.

A force-nine gale was blowing. People started to vomit as soon as the boat left the harbour. The stench was overpowering. Deirdre said she couldn't bear it. She needed a blow of fresh air. I catnapped and eventually fell asleep. I slept for more than an hour. There was no sign of Deirdre. I went to look for her. Passing a bar I thought I saw her white swagger coat. But when I pushed open the door the smell of stout hit me like a malodorous wave and I let the door close.

Here and there as I wandered about the ship, now and then steadying myself against the walls as it lurched, I saw girls we had boarded with and asked if they'd seen Deirdre. No one had. Eventually I reached the deck. The wind screeched and spray washed over the boat's side, fell onto the deck and drained into the scuppers. Maybe, I thought, Deirdre had fallen overboard. I'd have to find a seaman and report her missing. I found the wind exhilarating. The fresh, salt-laden air was gorgeous after the revolting smells in the lounge. Now and then I stopped my lurching along to lean over the vessel's side and watch the wake of the ship spin out behind it like yards of silk, a frothing mass of white in the darkness of the night.

There were other people leaning over the rail. I heard a man retch, but knowing nothing about the wind's direction I stayed where I was until a plaster of his vomit blew onto my cheek. My stomach turned and I almost threw up. I took several deep breaths, moved far from him, then took my scarf, already wet with spume, and wiped my face. I let the wind take the stinking scarf, wet a handkerchief in the scuppers and scrubbed my cheek and then let the handkerchief follow the scarf. All thoughts of a drowned Deirdre had left my mind. I was cold. I'd have to go back inside or find a sheltered place. The walking warmed me and once again I began to enjoy the storm, feel courageous braving the elements, let myself go with the pitch and roll of the ship, convincing myself I was a natural-born sailor. I was beginning a new life. A marvellous, exciting life. For wasn't it the middle of the night, dark, stormy, and I savouring every minute of it? I remembered heroines I'd read of who'd been connected with the sea ... Grace Darling, Gráinne. Gráinne sailing with her father, an O'Malley, a slip of a girl. A pirate plundering the ships of her enemies, and Grace risking her life to save the lives of others. I could be such a woman. There was nothing I couldn't do. I stood gazing at the tumultuous sea lost in my fantasies, my hair clinging to my skull, water dripping into my eyes, the shoulders and front of my coat saturated. I began again to shiver. But knew that I didn't want to go back to the crowded saloon, smoke-filled and reeking of vomit. Not yet, anyway. I walked again looking for shelter and came near the funnels. Behind one I'd be out of the wind and warm. I moved closer and then I saw them. A couple. A man and a woman. Her white coat and other clothes above her waist. The man holding her.

I could hear him grunting as he appeared to be trying to push her through the funnel's side. I had a vague idea of what they were doing. I was certain the woman was Deirdre and instinctively knew neither would welcome a greeting.

I made my way back, pushed open the heavy doors telling myself I would have to endure the lounge. Exhausted by this time, I fell asleep squashed between a man and a woman reeking of porter and slept until the boat docked. There was great activity. People looking for children, cases, and trying to guess where the gangplank would be attached to the ship. I met up with the girls who were travelling with me to join the ATS. Then Deirdre pushed her way through the throng and berated me. 'I've been looking for you all night.' She smelled of drink. 'I was worried and after me promising your mother I'd mind you. Will I get you a cup of tea, they're still open?'

'That'd be grand,' I said and watched her go, seeing at the same time in my mind's eye the white coat hoisted above her waist. She brought the tea. We waited to disembark. She didn't say any more about her search for me. And I said nothing about my stroll on deck.

'Right then, let's be having you,' Edith's voice put an end to my thoughts about Deirdre's escapade. 'Let's get a bit of shape on these bloody uniforms.'

'Let's leave it till after tea,' Marj suggested, and several voices agreed with her.

'We could do a lot in an hour,' Edith said, but she was outvoted. We lounged and smoked and talked. Mostly about food. The English girls longingly recalled meals before the war. The roast Sunday dinners, home-made steak and kidney pies with suet crusts, liver smothered in onions, real eggs, banana sandwiches, tomato sandwiches, oranges, and bacon butties with lashings of tomato sauce.

In Ireland only tea was strictly rationed, and I'd only left Dublin four days ago, so neither I nor the other Irish girls expressed longings. Though I did think how nice two lightly boiled eggs and a fresh Vienna roll would be at the moment.

The English girls were remembering when sweets weren't rationed. How every time they had money they bought sweets and chocolate. Crunchie bars and Tiffin bars, Fry's Cream chocolate, acid drops, Dolly mixtures, Liquorice Allsorts and sticks of liquorice. They went on remembering and planning what they'd buy when rationing ended.

The teatime meal differed only slightly from breakfast. A cube of butter and a dessert-spoonful of jam instead of margarine and marmalade. We went to the cookhouse carrying our knife, fork, spoon and enamel mug. There, with the other squads in training, we queued for the counter where vegetables and stews were served. One of the first things I noticed about some of the food was how it differed in colour from food at home. Greens, as they were called, hadn't a trace of green about them but were a blend of yellow, white and grey. Brown gravy was a shade I would have described as buff, beige or fawn. Brown stews were brown but with the first mouthful your palate recognized the artificial flavour. And when on rare occasions roast beef, pork or lamb was served, it too was a colour I didn't associate with such meats and was tough, fatty, full of gristle and tasteless.

For tea we were served 'toad in the hole': two sausages buried in a mass of doughy batter. I had never before seen such a dish. It was something my mother would have described as a plocky dollop. But hunger is good sauce. And we were hungry. We refilled our mugs with tea to take back to the barrack room while a khaki-overalled orderly, whose curlers made lumpy bumps beneath her turban, waited to remove the urn. Outside the cookhouse we washed our cutlery in the barrel of hot water provided, its surface shiny with grease. Preparations for the bulling of the uniforms began as soon as we were back in our room. 'Right, then,' said Edith, 'someone put the ironing board up. Get out your brasso, shoe polish, button sticks and two sanitary towels.'

'Sanitary towels, what for?' asked someone.

'For putting on the brasso and polish. You'll want your dusters and brushes, shoe and button ones, as well.'

Sanitary towels were Lord Nuffield's gift to the Women's Services. They were expensive to buy. At home many girls used rags. Washed and re-washed for many months. Sanitary towels were a luxury item and I'd never known them to be used except for the purpose for which they were intended. But soon I became used to ripping them apart, using the cotton wool for applying brasso, polish, cosmetics, cleaning windows. Once, many years after joining up, I visited a soldier in hospital who had had a throat operation. Around the wound on his neck and draped by the loops over his ears was a sanitary towel. He hadn't long come from the recovery room and so probably wasn't aware of the incongruous dressing. I was mortified with embarrassment for both of us. And at the same time wanted to giggle.

* * *

Edith showed us how to spit and polish. A mouthful of spittle into the Kiwi Dark Tan, a ball of cotton wool to blend the two. Then the corner of a cloth wound round the index finger, dipped into the tin, and then the tedious circling and circling of the shoe's surface, from time to time moistening the polish again or spitting directly onto the leather until the faintest of shines appeared.

'You're lucky you aren't blokes,' said Edith, pausing to inspect our achievements. 'You should see the men's boots the first time they're issued. Rough as a badger's arse they are. Have to be soaked in piss.'

Not sure if this wasn't another Paddy joke, I gave her a quizzical look.

'No kidding. I've seen new boots and me Dad told me. Keep a bucket in the barrack room and piss in it then dunk the boots. Softens and brings the leather up a treat.'

I spat, circled and rubbed until my arm ached and my finger felt paralysed. Everyone felt the same and we decided to call a halt.

Corporal Robinson came into the barrack room and enquired if we were all right. After she left I said how pleasant she seemed. Edith contradicted me. 'Wait'll she gets you on the square, it'll be a different story. She's still treating you like a civvy. Wait'll she gets you in uniform.'

The uniform. Momentarily I'd forgotten it. Forgotten my bitter disappointment on the day my kit was issued. A mountain of it. More clothes than I had ever possessed in my life. Three brassières, two corset belts, three pairs of khaki Directoire knickers—the ones Edith called 'wrist-stranglers'—three pairs of short white woollen panties, two pairs of blue-and-white striped flannel pyjamas, three pairs of thick stockings the colour of diarrhoea. Two pairs of shoes, one pair of plimsolls, baggy brown shorts, a burnt-orange shapeless sports shirt with a brown trim. Needles, threads, buttons in a small cotton bag called a 'husive'. Shirts with separate collars, a khaki woollen long-sleeved v-necked pullover, cap, jacket, tunic, skirt and greatcoat.

The uniform looked as if it had been made from a rough woollen blanket, and bore no more resemblance to the girl's uniform in the recruiting poster than I to her. I had fervently believed that, wearing what she was wearing, I would be transformed. I would go home to Ireland and dazzle my love. Now I imagined the sight I'd be. The rough thick cloth, no perky little cap. The ones we'd been issued had brims and yards of sticking-up crown. And all the shade of the vile stockings.

A lump rose in my throat. And in seconds I was crying out loud. I'd done it all for nothing. There would be no triumphant return to Dublin in a glamorous outfit. With my tail between my legs I'd go back in the green tweed coat for I wouldn't be seen dead in that tunic, skirt and cap. Soon I had a crowd round me. Everyone full of concern as I tried between hysterical sobs to tell Edith of the tragedy that had befallen me. 'I thought I'd look lovely. And then he'd notice me. And fall for me. He would, I know he would.'

Out I blurted everything. About the poster and the one I loved for so long. My one and only reason for joining up.

'Pad,' she said, 'you're daft as a bleeding brush. Haven't you ever heard of de Valera?'

'What's he got to do with it?' I asked, sobs still threatening to choke me.

'He's that long drink of water with the specs.'

'I know what he looks like.'

'Yeah, well, he's the one who wouldn't let us have your ports. Kept you out of the war. Ireland's neutral. So even if the uniform was a dead ringer for the one in the magazine you still couldn't wear it.'

'But why?' I persisted.

'You can't wear the uniform of a country at war, in a neutral one. You could be shot. Slung in prison camp.'

'Are you sure?'

'Positive. And listen, kid, forget about the fella. You'll meet hundreds over here in the army camps. Fighting them off you'll be.'

'So I joined up for nothing,' I said, pity again welling up in me.

'You joined up for the same reason we all did. Nothing to do with fellas. You were fed up at home. You were fed up being under your Mam's thumb. You wanted change, adventure. And you've got us. We're mates, all mates, OK? I'll put a bit of shape on your uniform, you won't know it.'

'By tomorrow?' I asked doubtfully.

'That was a mistake. Someone read the Part Two Orders wrong. One of your lot. So we've all tomorrow for sorting out the uniforms.' She yawned. 'I'm whacked. Get ready for bed. Have a fag first and no more bawling. Right?'

With a degree of modesty the girls had begun undressing, putting on their striped pyjamas. I'd never had an abundant supply of nightwear at home. Even so I hated the army pyjamas. Too long, too loose, especially the jacket, which was like an overcoat in length. Then Bubbles had an idea. She undid the pyjamas' bottom buttons, brought up the two ends and tied them just above her navel. Then folded the surplus back material to fit tidily behind. 'Smashing,' we chorused.

'Who showed you how to do that?' someone asked.

'At the pictures. An American girl's college or beach. I can't remember.' In minutes we had all copied Bubbles and in the future always tied up our pyjamas.

* * *

Edith borrowed an enamel plate from an orderly in the cookhouse, and from somewhere else had got hold of a cloth to use for pressing, a bucket of water and a sliver of soap. She demonstrated how a good pressing reduced the rough appearance of the uniform. How to run the sliver of soap along where the crease in the skirt should be, then turn it on its right side and bang away with the iron. The crease was knife-like. The plate was fitted into the crown of the cap, the surplus material that stood up pinched and pleated around its edge. It was an improvement, I had to admit. But still I hated the uniform and always would.

We polished our detachable leather cap bands and the cap badges, and then, careful not to crease the tunic, gathered the buttons into the button stick. An attractive thing made from solid brass, divided in its centre so that the buttons could be slipped into it and polished without fear of metal polish spoiling the cloth.

The atmosphere that evening was a happy, expectant one. For the following day after tea we would be allowed to leave the camp for the first time. We pushed to the backs of our minds our first experience of drill in the morning. For days, as we'd nursed our sore arms and marked and prepared our kit through the open window, we had heard and seen other squads being put through their paces. The drill corporal marched up and down shouting commands. 'Right turn, Left turn, About turn, Forward march. Swing those arms shoulder-high.' Occasionally they called words of praise. 'Well done, C Squad,' or whichever squad hadn't made a balls-up of their drill movements.

We speculated as to how we would spend our first evening away from camp.

One of the English girls said, 'Maybe we'll see blokes. Haven't seen a man since I came here.'

'It's a women's training camp, that's why. Once we're posted you'll be falling over them,' someone else explained.

'Let's hope you're right. That's why I joined up. Not a decent-looking man where I live. Women, kids and old men. I wonder where we'll be posted?' the first girl said.

Edith answered her. 'Not where you want to go, cock. They give you a choice. You ask for Scotland and you'll finish up in Devon.'

I knew where I wanted to go when basic training was finished. To Brighton, where my father had come from. I'd look up his relations. His father was still alive. I'd meet him. The majority of the Irish girls hoped for posting to London, Birmingham and Coventry, being familiar with the names of these cities where their fathers, brothers and relations had worked during the war. Deirdre expressed no preference. The girls from England talked of Aldershot, Colchester and other army camps, where the ratio of men to women made the getting of a fella 'dead easy'.

An English girl who hadn't so far taken part in the discussion said, 'I want to go where there's Yanks. I think they're smashing.'

Someone informed her that Americans were stationed at Burton Wood and they came into the local town every night. She'd be bound to see them the next evening. There were whoops of glee.

'On the make,' a cynical voice said.

The girl who first mentioned Yanks replied, 'They can make me anytime.'

'So long as it isn't pregnant,' the cynic said. 'Get yourself in "the club", the Yank vanishes.'

'Our kid's engaged to one,' Marj said. 'She's going to be a GI bride. Smashing he is. You should see what he brings her from the PX store. Boxes of chewing gum, cartons of fags, chocolates, tins of food for me Mam, and nylons.'

'Nylons!' There were gasps of envious admiration.

'Mean cow, our kid. She wouldn't lend us a pair, never mind give us one. She has to have all sorts of tests before they get married, for TB and VD. You have to fill in that many forms, even who your granny was. He's got a ranch, her fella has.'

'I hope it's not a gopher ranch,' said Edith.

'She never said anything about gophers. What are they when they're at home, a kind of cow?'

'I don't know,' Edith admitted. 'Only sometimes I heard the Yanks in our local talk about gopher ranches and nearly kill themselves laughing.'

'I'd love to live in California,' said Bubbles. 'Tomorrow night I'll keep my eyes out for a Yank.'

The cynic joined in again, saying all Yanks were hot stuff.

Bubbles smiled an enigmatic smile and Deirdre spoke for the first time. 'I'd like to see any Yank try to get fresh with me. He'd live to regret it.' I listened and thought of her pressed against the ship's funnel with the white swagger above her waist.

* * *

Later on we talked of the jobs we'd like to do when basic training finished. Bubbles wanted to drive a Staff Car. 'Land a wealthy old Brigadier,' she said flippantly. 'I think that's what I'll apply for,' I said. 'Driving would be great.' Another recruit wanted to join ack-ack battery, only to be reminded by several of the English girls that ack-ack sites were dangerous. Forty ATSs had been killed at one in Biggin Hill.

'Not much chance of that,' Edith disabused the girl with an ambition to shoot down enemy planes. 'The war's nearly over. Ack-ack batteries are being run down.'

Mess orderlies was the most popular choice. Marj extolled the perks. More food, able to keep curlers in as the khaki turban hid them. It was a bobby's job.

After the choice of jobs the English girls talked about the coming election. I knew nothing about politics, Irish or British, having only ever looked at the Dublin *Evening Herald* to follow the Mutt and Jeff cartoon. But many of the English girls bought the *Daily Mirror* and read with great interest news of the coming election. Pinning their hopes on a Labour victory, as were their families and the working-class people all over the country. With the Labour Party in power great things would happen. No more unemployment. No more panel doctors. Free false teeth, glasses. A share-out of everything. Churchill was alright during the war. But his day was over.

THREE

The next morning, dressed in my uniform, I looked in the barrack room's full-length glass and wanted to cry. After all the pressing, soaping, spit, polish, enamel plate and pleating of the cap's crown it looked hideous. But I instinctively knew that even the good-natured Edith's patience would run out if at every disappointment I turned on the 'waterworks', as she called excessive crying.

I'd have to put up with the uniform, maybe find ways of improving it. The tunic was on the big side. Shifting the buttons would help. That could wait until later. But something had to be done about my hair, which hung lankly, resting on my collar. I asked Edith's advice. 'Two inches above your collar, that's regulations. You could be put on a fizzer for that.'

'What'll I do?'

'I'll give it a trim.'

'I'll fix it,' said Bubbles.

'Without cutting?' I didn't want my hair cut; I was planning that when I had enough money I'd get a perm. With curls and waves and my teeth, which I knew were beautiful, I'd be presentable.

'No cutting,' Bubbles assured me, smiling like a knowing cherub with her blonde hair curling round her cap. 'Hang on, I'll get my spare shoelaces.' She did, knotted them, placed the ring on my head, and strand by strand rolled my hair round them, tucking every straggling hair securely in. The front she brushed into three sweeps, fixed one over each ear and one above my forehead. An unbecoming hairstyle except for the exceptionally pretty. But it was tidy and two inches above my collar and after five minutes on the square I forgot about my appearance as I attempted to learn the drill manoeuvres. Remember which was my left foot, my right arm, keep in step, not bring the wrathful voice of Corporal Robinson singling me out.

We marched up and down, wheeled and about-turned, some making the turn so that they faced each other and were tongue-lashed by the immaculate Robinson. My legs felt leaden, my too-tight cap band made my head ache. The brassière I had longed for and was wearing for the first time restricted my chest without supporting my breasts. I didn't like drill and knew at my first session that I never would.

At last we were commanded to halt, stand to attention, stand at ease, fall out. We were free. Free to go to the barrack room, the lavatory, and have a quick smoke. 'Half an hour,' said Edith, 'half a bloody hour. My feet are killing me.' Everyone had a moan. Each of us in turn had been inspected before drilling began. And each of us in turn had been found wanting. Crumpled collars, dull buttons, caps not sitting straight on the head. All the offences were minor except Deirdre's. The eagle eye of the Corporal had noticed the absence from Deirdre's left tunic pocket of her AB64, a brown booklet with our physical description, including distinguishing facial marks. There was a section in which we named our next of kin, could make a will, a page listing the injections we had received, and many more pages that as yet meant nothing to the new recruits.

The little brown book was our most important document. And never must we move outside the barrack room without it in our possession. When we were not in uniform it would be carried in our khaki canvas shoulder-bag; when in uniform we carried it in our left breast tunic pocket. It was a serious offence to disobey this rule, a chargeable offence, but as a new recruit Deirdre escaped with a telling off.

The break was up. Those who had lit a second cigarette nipped them and saved the butts. The next stop was the dentist, where appointments were made for treatment. Then another break. A wonderful interlude in the cookhouse where we were served milky sweet cocoa and currant buns and told that this was the time of day when in future our mail would be distributed. We drank and ate, talked and smoked. Saw the drill session as something to be endured, hoped we'd improve. Our good humour was restored. Before leaving the cookhouse a list was taken of those not yet eighteen who, if and when a ration of bananas became available, would be entitled to one. During the six weeks in basic training the bananas never materialized.

Before dinner we attended a lecture on current affairs. I listened attentively but the lectures meant little to me. And in any case my thoughts were on the coming evening.

After dinner we were having physical training. 'More square-bashing,' said Edith, standing in the baggy rayon shorts that creased as you looked at them, plimsolls, no socks, and tangerine sports shirt.

We grumbled about everything: the uniform, food, NCOs, regulations. But there was always something to laugh at. Usually the officers and NCOs; the bellowing of the latter and plummy voices of the former. Laughing at yourself as you remembered the fools you must have seemed, not able to tell your right foot from your left. And that day our good humour was almost manic, keyed up as we were with the prospect of our freedom after tea when we'd be let loose on the town.

* * *

Physical training wasn't anything like drill. At the gymnasium we were greeted by Corporal Barret, our instructor. Her voice was sweet and welcoming as she explained that PT was a gentle, relaxing form of exercise. Very good for us. It was enjoyable and would improve our posture and general health. 'It's great fun, actually. After we've warmed up I'll demonstrate the exercises, which you will then copy.'

I listened spellbound, in thrall not to her words but to her appearance. The pale blue aertex shirt, short shorts, golden-brown face, arms and legs. Neat white ankle socks, soft leather shoes as flexible as dancing slippers. Around her neck she wore a snowy white lanyard from which hung a whistle that to my bemused eyes could have been solid silver.

There and then I made a decision. One day, no matter what it took, I would be a PTI.

* * *

We huddled in a group like ragamuffins, awkward and embarrassed. Though probably not Bubbles. Bubbles was posh. Bubbles had poise. As yet I wasn't familiar with the term, but

Bubbles, like the instructor, Corporal Robinson and most of the officers, was middle class.

We the hoi-polloi shuffled and cleared our throats, hiked up our brassière's shoulder straps and giggled nervously as we eyed the immaculately dressed instructor. 'Now girls,' she said, 'move apart. In a circle round the gym. Fine. Good. That's it.' We shifted, spaced ourselves and made a circle, into which she entered, placing herself in its centre. Then she lifted an arm and pointed, and in a voice with no semblance of the drill instructor's bark commanded, 'Running this way round, run.' We ran. Some of us ran so enthusiastically that we trod on the heels of laggards. 'Like a lot of bloody kids in school,' Edith said, stopping to pull up her plimsoll's trodden-down heel, causing more collisions and peals of laughter.

We were, in fact, like kids in school and it was wonderful. Playing in the afternoon. Which I suppose, with the exception of Bubbles, none of us had done since leaving school. For once you went to work at fourteen, as most of us had, playing was a thing of the past. I never knew anyone in the clothing factory who played tennis. Tennis clubs were not for us and as far as I knew there were no public courts. Some of my better-off relations fenced. But on the whole the recreation of poor girls was dancing once a week, where the attendance wasn't for the exercise but in the hopes of finding a fella.

Half an hour of rhythmic exercises, throwing and catching bean-bags and balls. Bending and stretching to reduce hips, thighs and bellies. Our movements were encouraged and, when necessary, corrected by the instructress. All too soon the session ended with a posture-improving technique. We tucked in our tails, dropped our shoulders, stood tall and didn't allow our chins to poke forward. Walking back to my billet the instructress passed wearing a most becoming track suit. And again I told myself, 'That's what I'm going to be, a PTI.'

FOUR

A communal shower followed the physical training session. Bare breasts no longer amazed me. I joined in with the singing of the gypsy song and learned a version of 'She'll be coming round the mountain when she comes' which I'd never heard before.

Back in uniform we attended a lecture on King's Regulation. I paid little attention, my mind being occupied wondering what qualifications I would need to be a PTI. We smoked. Smoking was allowed almost everywhere. Smoking was encouraged by a duty-free allowance of cigarettes.

The ATS officer was talking about privileges. I began to listen. She sounded like Corporal Robinson and Bubbles. Bubbles came from Liverpool, Robinson from London, and the officer probably from some other part of England. It puzzled me, the similarity of their voices. And I thought it wasn't so in Ireland. Even with educated people you could still recognize their regional accent. No one would be described as talking as if they had a plum in their mouth.

'You are entitled to food, accommodation, a certain amount of free laundry and facilities for cleanliness.'

An English girl put her hand up. 'Ma'am,' she asked when given permission to speak, 'What about pay, ma'am?'

'That is also a privilege. It can be reduced or stopped for certain offences.' And suddenly I remembered the allowance, the allowance for my mother. I had forgotten all about it. I whispered this to Marj. 'Too late now, cock,' she whispered back. 'By the time this lot's finished the Company Office will be shut. See about it in the morning.'

* * *

We were getting ready to go to town. The atmosphere was charged with nervous excitement. Stubs of lipstick were borrowed. Bubbles, the only one with a bottle of scent, generously dabbed it behind our ears. Advice and help were given on hairstyles and at which angle the flat cap would look the most becoming. Everyone was speculating as to how they would spend the evening. Edith, Marj and Bubbles elected to go to the public house. The idea tempted me. Mostly because I would have preferred their company to Deirdre's, but also because I had never been inside a public house. In Ireland respectable young women might cross the threshold of one to present a jug discreetly to the barman, who filled it with stout for your granny or mother. But my mother didn't drink stout. 'It never passed my lips,' she often proclaimed, 'not even when after my births I was ordered it by the Master of the Coombe Hospital.' At Christmas, weddings and christenings she would take a sherry or port. And I didn't have a granny so going into a public house appealed to my curiosity and a new-found sense of freedom and daring.

'I might come with you,' I said to Edith, 'if that's OK.'

'Do,' she replied, 'pubs are the best place for getting fellas.'

'You will not,' said Deirdre. 'I made a promise to your mother. We'll go to the pictures.'

Already I had found her tedious. Like a limpet she clung to me. She was too old for me. I never got a laugh out of her. But sometimes in the midst of so many country, Lancashire and Cheshire accents I found her Dublin one comforting. I appealed to Edith, 'Deirdre could come to the pub as well, couldn't she?'

'I couldn't care less who comes—it's a free country,' Edith said. I didn't think it was the most welcoming of invitations. But I wasn't surprised. Edith and Deirdre sniped at each other. Deirdre objected to being called Paddy. 'I was christened and it wasn't Paddy,' she would remind Edith when accidentally on purpose she used the nickname.

'I wouldn't be found dead in a public house,' Deirdre retorted, pausing in the arranging of her lovely dark hair before the mirror.

'Suit yourself, cock,' said Edith.

'And you're not going either,' she said to me. 'You heard your mother at the station. I hope you haven't forgotten I'm minding you.'

33

'I haven't forgotten,' I said, and thought of how well she had minded me on the boat, the smell of drink on her breath when she eventually came back and pretended to find me. 'But I'd like to go and my mother won't know,' I argued.

'You can't anyway. You're not twenty-one.'

'I wasn't going to drink,' I protested feebly, 'just to have a look.'

She threatened to write and tell my mother and I agreed to the pictures.

There was much speculation amongst us as to whether we might get off with Yanks. Would we be safe with them if we did?

'They're only men,' Bubbles said reassuringly. But the majority of the Irish girls (including me) had never been out alone with a man. I didn't count the one who had picked me up one night as I walked home late from a relation's house. He was on a bike, slowed down and stopped when he came abreast of me. He said it was a grand night and I said it was. We walked along, him pushing his bicycle in the gutter. Passed the cemetery where my father was buried. I blessed myself and said a little silent prayer. And as we walked he told me he worked for a milkman. That one day he hoped to have his own round. I asked him if he liked being a milkman. He said it was a job but that he had wanted to join the British army and be a paratrooper. I asked him why he hadn't. 'Me ma didn't want me to go, she's a widow and I'm the only son. But in any case I have a disability so I don't suppose they'd have taken me.' I wasn't sure what a disability meant and didn't like to ask.

I told him where I worked, that my father was dead, and that I had a brother and sister. He had a nice manner and I enjoyed talking to him. We exchanged names. I didn't notice at the time that he never turned his head to look me full in the face. Just kept talking and pushing his bicycle along the gutter.

Just before we came to a junction in the road, he said, 'I was wondering if you'd come to the pictures on Saturday night, there's a good one in the Savoy.' I didn't know how to refuse. He seemed nice anyway and I'd be able to boast in work that I had a fella and was going with him to the Savoy. So, I said, 'Thanks very much, that'd be grand.' We arrived at the junction and he said, 'This is where I'll have to turn off. See you on Saturday,' and, still without turning to look at me, swung his leg over the saddle and rode off.

I wasn't sure if I'd recognize him amongst all the men waiting outside the cinema. But he called my name and came towards me and I nearly died of embarrassment. He only had one eye. Not one and a glass one: one eye and an empty socket. All I could think of was someone I knew from work seeing me with him. A fella with only one eye. But I didn't have the nerve, or maybe it was the heart, to walk away and leave him. He had bought good seats and chocolates for me. I kept praying for the lights to go down. But even in the dark I kept thinking of the time when they'd come up again.

I lied and said it was a smashing picture though I had watched almost none of it. We crossed the street to where he had left his bicycle. He never spoke about the eye that was missing, and I thanked God that no one I knew had been around. He asked if I'd meet him again, same place, same time next week, and I agreed, not knowing how to refuse but knowing that I wouldn't turn up.

I made a joke of it to the girls in work. Everyone including me laughed about my 'blind date'. For a while I was racked with guilt and never walked home from my relation's the way I had when I met him. And fervently hoped I'd never bump into him again.

* * *

I took a long look at myself in the full-length mirror before leaving the barrack room and decided that in spite of the pressing, primping and titivating I looked awful. 'Oh God, I hate these stockings, they're like an old woman's, and look at my collar, it's curled up already.'

'Stop moaning,' said Edith. 'During the week buy the fully fashioned ones in the Scotch Wool Shop. You can afford the coupons, being Irish.'

'We only get the same number as you,' said Deirdre.

'Aye, but your clothes in Ireland are not as strictly rationed as ours. And in any case I was talking to Paddy. She's got gorgeous legs. Not like some,' and she let her eyes travel the length of what was to be seen of Deirdre's, which in Ireland would have been described as 'beef to the heels like a Mullingar heifer'.

When I was little my mother used to tell me that I had fine limbs while forcing cod liver oil and Parish's food down my throat. The nuns in the school told me I wore my dresses too short and one pinned a paper hem around my fine limbs. But no one had remarked on my legs since I had grown up. The compliment lifted my spirit. And I told myself I would buy the fully fashioned stocking even though other ranks were forbidden to wear them. And send my collars to the Chinese laundry which made them stiff and shiny.

* * *

All my life I had believed that everywhere in England was beautiful. That unlike Dublin there were no slums and no poor people. My mother had read me *The Old Curiosity Shop* and I cried over Little Nell and her grandfather. But that was a story about the olden days. My views of England had been formed by my father's descriptions of Brighton, Hove, Beachy Head and London. I had seen the Pathé News of the Coronation. Read Angela Brazil. Stories of girls in boarding schools, midnight feasts, tennis and lacrosse.

And for final proof, there were many people from our neighbourhood who had gone to work in England and prospered. They came home for holidays dressed to the nines with pockets full of money which they lavishly spent. Talked about the grand houses or flats they lived in and praised England whenever they spoke of it.

So my first sight of an English town was a bitter disappointment. Even the glorious sunset could do little to enhance the grimy buildings, the run-down houses. Small houses. Little shops. Low-sized people poorly dressed. And everywhere a smell of smoke. But as Deirdre and I walked on towards the town and I paid more attention to the passing people rather than buildings, many smiled at me, some commented on the fine evening. They were friendly and welcoming. They reminded me of Dubliners, many with humorous faces and laughter in their eyes.

And then coming towards us were Yanks. I recognized them from the films I'd seen of American soldiers. They were so clean, so well groomed in uniforms that appeared to have been made to measure. Such a contrast to the soldiers we had seen in Belfast and on the train and platforms we had passed on our way to Cheshire. English soldiers in hairy khaki battle-dress either too tight or too baggy.

The Yanks said 'Hi,' smiled, chewed gum. Real Americans

talking in an accent we had only ever heard at the pictures.

They passed by. Deirdre and I began to talk. 'From America,' she said, 'real Americans. From the same place as Clark Gable, Frank Sinatra. And did you see the two-tone uniforms? The lovely olive-green tunic and pinky-beige trousers? Some of them might even be film stars.'

'They're gorgeous.'

'But don't forget they're supposed to be fast,' Deirdre said. 'I'd never go out with them. I'd be afraid of my life.'

She sounded so genuinely fearful I wondered if perhaps I had imagined the scene on the deck. Or could the girl with the white swagger hoisted above her waist have been someone else? White swagger coats weren't uncommon.

We were nearing a railway bridge and could hear a train. We leant over the bridge to watch the train and hadn't been there long when two American soldiers came and stood beside us. They seemed very old to me. About thirty I guessed. They bid us 'Good evening', and when the train had passed under the bridge they introduced themselves as Lewis and Paul, both from Philadelphia. They asked what branch of the Services we were in. Deirdre did all the talking. Her face became vivacious as she answered their questions, smiling, her eyes with a light in them that I didn't remember seeing before. She told them our names, that we were from Ireland. Paul laughed and said he guessed as much. I was tongue-tied until Lewis suggested we might like to walk a little way with them and have a drink or coffee.

'We can't. We're going to the pictures.' Nervousness wouldn't let me stop. 'To see *State Fair*. Judy Garland's in it. It's supposed to be very good.'

'We could take you,' Lewis said. 'It's a great film.'

And off I went again. 'Oh, no. Thanks very much. What I meant to say is that we were thinking about going. It all depends on what time the picture finishes. D'ye see, we have to be back in barracks by ten-thirty. That's when we have to check in. If we didn't we could be on a fizzer, that's a charge, you know.'

Deirdre was looking daggers at me. Lewis suggested we walk to the cinema and check when the performance finished. And my minder, the Judas, said she thought that was a great idea. I could tell by the excitement in her voice, in her eyes, in how she moved her stout body, pushing out her chest, tilting her head to one side, that she was determined to go along with the Yanks

37

and if I refused I'd be dumped in a town where I knew no one. So I went with them, dreading the thought of being with two Americans in a dark picture house, wishing I had gone to the public house with Edith and the crowd.

Deirdre walked ahead with Paul, who looked younger than Lewis. As we followed them Lewis asked questions about Dublin, about the town we were in. What was its population, its main industries? In my later experiences with Americans I found that many asked the same questions. Using the slang I was picking up, I replied, 'I haven't a clue.'

He offered me a cigarette. I smoked very little then and never in the street. I refused and when he lit up thanked God that I had. For it smelled like no cigarette I had ever smelled.

My mother's warnings sounded in my mind. Drugged cigarettes and drinks, rape and white slave traffic. I longed to be safe in Dublin, in the barrack room. Anywhere but approaching the picture house with an American I had just met. Deirdre and Paul reached the cinema before us and were reading the times of performances and looking at the stills. Paul said, 'It's OK. Finishes at quarter of ten.' Deirdre was all smiles. She squeezed my arm as we went into the foyer. When the Yanks came from the box office, she took the cigarettes they offered. That smell again and the name, Camels, conjured up a desert scene, sheikhs and dancing girls, slaves, white girls abducted and sold into slavery. But I kept telling myself, 'So long as you neither eat nor drink anything they offer you'll be alright.' I answered myself, 'You won't be drugged but supposing in the dark they try other things? I'll scream the place down so I will.'

They had bought the most expensive seats. Our row filled up and before the lights went down I saw the other rows were also full. Some Yanks, but many civilian men and women. I told myself they would come to my rescue if anything terrible happened. Nothing did. Not a hand brushed near me. Gradually I relaxed and soon was lost in the picture. Lost so completely I never even glanced at the cinema clock. But Lewis did and whispered, startling me, 'It's nearly over and you're OK for time.' They walked us back, stopping only to buy us a dozen doughnuts each from the American Doughnut dug-out. It was almost dark and the street lamps lit when we turned into the road leading to the barracks. It was surrounded by a high brick wall which ran for a considerable length. Along the wall Yanks and ATS girls were in passionate embraces. I couldn't believe my eyes. Never in my life had I seen such a thing. People kissing in public. Not pecks on cheeks but lips on lips and bodies close to each other.

'They've got no shame,' said Deirdre in a scandalized voice. I hoped the spectacle along the wall wouldn't put ideas into Paul and Lewis's heads. It didn't. Very politely they thanked us for our company and bid us goodnight.

Clutching our bags of still-warm doughnuts we reported to the guardroom, were marked in and proceeded to the barrack room. On the way Deirdre said, 'Oul' fellas they were. I wouldn't have gone out with them again, not if they'd gone down on bended knees. But let on they asked and we refused.'

Edith, Marj and Bubbles were already in, giggling and in high spirits. They regaled us with the good time they'd had in the public house. 'It were smashing, Pad. You should have come. Bubbles got off with a Yank and me and Marj ...' Deirdre interrupted. 'So did we, two officers. Wanted to take us to Chester for the weekend. But we said no. The pictures is one thing but a weekend is another.'

'They bought us these.' I held out the doughnuts. Twelve to a bag. One for each of us. Everyone was ravenous. Late at night we always were. Our sweet ration was already gone, eaten on the day we got it. Tea had been served at five o'clock. As it was a camp run by women the cooks sometimes managed to put up a meagre supper from the daily rations. A few Spam or bully-beef sandwiches and cocoa. It was first come first served and most nights during our training we went to bed hungry. As a consolation Edith had warned us that when we were posted out, if it was a camp where men were in charge of catering we'd go hungry every night. No supper in a male cookhouse. The men were all on the fiddle. Single cooks sold any surplus and married ones took it home.

The doughnuts were devoured. We licked every last grain of sugar from our fingers, then got ready for bed. And talked about tomorrow, drill, me about going to the office to apply for the dependant's allowance. And I mentioned the Yanks and girls along the barrack wall. Bubbles said it was commonplace now wherever there were Yanks, and now the English chaps were copying them. Everyone was in bed by lights-out.

Talking continued for a while. I could hear Deirdre saying her prayers. Hail Marys, Our Fathers and a litany of prayers for the dead. 'Sacred Heart of Jesus, have mercy on my father, my granny, Auntie Mary and Maggie, Uncle Jack, Mrs Behan.' On and on and on until she must have run out of names or fallen asleep. In a low voice someone far down the room hummed bars of 'Meet Me in Saint Louis, Louis, Meet Me at the Fair', the theme song from the film. Then it was all quiet.

It was a warm night, the moon shone through the curtainless windows. I thought of how happy I was. How much I liked the Forces. Sleeping in a barrack room. How the horrible uniform didn't matter, for soon I would be a Physical Training Instructor. Then faraway I heard the sound of a train, a lonely sad sound, and suddenly I too was sad. Overwhelmed with a longing to be at home, sitting round the table in our kitchen with my mother, brother and sister. The green-painted dresser with some of my mother's cracked and stitched antique plates on it. They'd be drinking tea and eating dark crusted bread well spread with butter. Now and then my mother giving orders for the wireless to be turned up if she was about to ballyrag the neighbour who she believed could hear every word because she had removed several bricks from her wall for that purpose. They'd argue, my sister contradicting my mother, but most of all there'd be a lot of laughter.

I wondered if they'd talk about me. Were they missing me? Wishing I hadn't gone away? Only once before in my life had I been parted from them. I loved them so much. I missed them so much. Tears ran down my face. And then I remembered my mother's preparations for the night. The hearth had to be swept in, and the floor. For the house was infested with mice. Not a crumb must be left to encourage them.

In the bedroom, within her hand's reach, she kept a supply of old shoes which, when the light was out and the mice emboldened to creep from their holes, she hurled in their direction, making a growling noise at the same time.

I thought about how during the night, getting up to go to the lavatory, she'd forget about the strewn shoes, stub her toes or fall over them. Curse the mice to Hell's Gates and, if she'd forgotten to anoint us with Holy Water, do so as we were falling asleep for the second time while she liberally showered our faces with the Blessed Water asking God to protect her children and bring them safely through the night. I was probably smiling when I fell asleep.

FIVE

Perhaps it rained during the first three weeks of basic training, but I only remember long days of sunshine. I no longer dreaded drill parades. Turned left and right, about-turned, moved to the right in threes, swung my arms shoulder-high, came smartly to attention and could salute an officer in the required manner.

Physical training continued to delight me. Half-hourly sessions of rhythmic exercise designed to correct stooped shoulders, bulging bellies and large bums; plumb-lines against which you stood to improve your posture; and throughout the lessons the glamorous, suntanned instructor giving praise and encouragement. I watched and listened, storing the information for the day when I too would be an instructor.

My mind was also easy. I had applied for my mother's allowance, signed the forms, one of them compulsory, allowing my mother two and six a week to top up whatever monies she was granted. And I had written home, assuring her that any day now her allowance book would arrive.

Everything was wonderful. Such friends I had never known before. Warm-hearted, good-natured girls. Except for Bubbles, we owned few possessions, other than rosary beads, scapulars, prayer books and a few relics of saints belonging to the Irish girls. Few had watches, fountain pens, diaries or sponge bags and we had only the minimum of cosmetics. We shared stubs of lipsticks, and borrowed and lent pipe-cleaners and Dinkie curlers for our hair. The English girls shared their food parcels from home: cakes scarce of fruit made with dried eggs. We had midnight feasts reminding me of stories in *Girl's Own*.

Even the horrible uniform caused less heartache. Every night, in the way Edith had demonstrated, we folded our skirts.

Frequent pressing had flattened the surplus nap. The cap no longer resembled the hat of a hydrocephalic chef. And the Chinese laundry had wrought a miraculous transformation with our collars. Stiff and shiny and crease-resistant.

On pay-day we paraded and received our money, then dashed to the NAFFI to buy our fifty duty-free cigarettes, our sweet ration and whatever cleaning materials were about to run out. Brasso and Dark Tan Kiwi polish lasted no time.

After tea we went to town. The girls had formed cliques. Edith, Marj and Bubbles, except when her American officer was off duty, went to the public house. I knew I could have gone with them but my minder, Deirdre, reminded me of my confirmation pledge and her promise to my mother, so we walked the streets, where she endeavoured to click with the Yanks. Many got into talk with us, gave us Camels and gum, but it never went any further. Deirdre said it was my fault. 'You've got a terrible short manner, d'ye know that. We're just getting going and you come out with one of your jawbreakers and kill the whole thing dead.'

Without confiding my innermost thoughts and inadequacies to Deirdre, I couldn't explain my behaviour. Believing that no man could find me attractive, I drew on all the advice I'd read in women's magazines about intelligence and personality being more important than a retroussé nose, baby-blue eyes and curls. In an attempt to be interesting I introduced words I had learnt the meaning of from the *Reader's Digest*. I did frighten them off. And because they hunted in pairs, Deirdre, with her winning smile, simpering and giggling, was dumped along with me.

I made excuses to her that I didn't want to finish underneath the light by the barrack wall in the stranglehold of a Yank.

'Not much fear of that,' she retorted.

'Then go out with some of the others,' I suggested. 'I don't care.'

And I didn't, knowing there were many groups I could have gone about with, whereas, not being popular, she was stuck with me. There was something about her that nobody warmed to. She would forget to buy toothpaste, borrow cigarettes and then, when she had her ration, not offer it around. A host of little things were noted. And when Bubbles reported seeing her in the post office depositing money in a savings account, she was truly recognized for being a cadger.

Halfway through our training we were granted a seventy-two-hour pass with travel warrant and ration money. The girls from Lancashire and Cheshire were ecstatic. Three days at home. They whooped with joy. For the Irish girls it was a bleak prospect. Myself and Deirdre could just about make it to Dublin. But for anyone from rural Ireland the seventy-two-hour pass was a non-starter.

The English girls talked non-stop about the meals they would eat at home. Sleeping late in the mornings. Seeing their mams and dads who weren't in the forces. And I thought of three days without them. Without their laughter. Their songs. Imitations of Corporal Robinson and officers with plums in their mouths. Their discussions of the coming election and the wonderful world we would live in when a Labour government was in power. Even Sunday Mass wouldn't be the same, for often one or other of the English girls came with me and Deirdre, and was fascinated at the amount of kneeling, standing, sitting and genuflecting. And asked again and again what it was that the 'Father' put on our tongues when we knelt at the Communion rails.

* * *

My mother wrote asking what had happened to the allowance she was supposed to get and I replied 'any day now', explaining that my voluntary contribution of half a crown a week was being deducted from my pay. Then one morning while we were enjoying our milky cocoa and currant buns the mail orderly brought our letters. Mine was a long brown envelope. A bulky envelope addressed in my mother's handwriting. Hoping for a nice surprise, a pair of stockings, a couple of packets of cigarettes, sweets or letters from my brother and sister, I opened it, reached inside and pulled out what looked like an extra-long book of raffle tickets. Printed on the cover was my mother's name and address, and printed in the right-hand corner the figures two shillings and sixpence. I flicked through the pages. The same sum was printed on each page. I didn't know what to make of it until, delving into the envelope, I found a single sheet of copybook paper which read, 'If you think I'd go to the post office and belittle myself to cash half a crown you've another thing coming. May God forgive you for deserting your widowed mother. Leaving her destitute while you're flying your kite in England. And as for the allowance book you know what you can do with that.' She hadn't addressed me nor signed the note.

I wasn't hurt or annoyed. That's how my mother wrote and spoke when in a bad humour. But the allowance book puzzled me. The half a crown was what I was allowing her. What had happened to the one the army should have awarded her? While eating more of my currant bun and drinking cocoa I thought two books must be issued. My allowance and the army's. Yes, that had to be it. The allowance books had crossed in the post. I could see her regretting the snotty note, telling herself she shouldn't have been so hasty. I ate and drank some more, then doubts assailed me, so I asked advice of the oracle.

'Something wrong there, kid,' Edith said after studying the book. 'The allowance would have been lumped together. Nip round to the Company Office and ask the Sarge.'

The ATS Sergeant listened and examined the book. 'Ah yes,' she said. 'The claim was turned down. You would have been notified and a letter will be sent to your mother.'

'But why?' I asked.

'It wasn't considered justified.' She shrugged. 'No explanations are given.'

'Is there nothing I can do about it?'

'You can stop the voluntary contribution. If in the future your mother's circumstances worsen you can apply again. Otherwise you can do nothing.'

Half a crown a week. Well, it was better than nothing. In time my mother would realize that. But she'd let it run for several weeks. And verbally beat me round the head with accusations of never having applied for a dependant's allowance in the first place. And enjoy every minute of her accusations and my denials. It would be another drama. That's how she was, my warm-hearted, generous mother with a tongue like a knife. Never at a loss for the right word at the right moment. Cut and thrust, parry, riposte, and in the next breath she'd be telling me the news of the neighbourhood. Who had died. If it was a happy death or one where the dying did not go gently into that dark night. And in between feeding me lightly boiled eggs with fresh Vienna rolls or a duck loaf from the Jewish baker. .

* * *

In the barrack room after dinner I held forth about the army not granting the money. And one of the Irish girls asked, 'What did you put on the form?'

'The truth. You know, that my mother is a widow and I was the only one earning. And how much I gave her.'

'That's why she didn't get it, because you told the truth. The army'd look at it this way. You weren't giving your mother much money. They'd reckon she'd probably be better off not having to keep you. Work out how much you ate, wear and tear on bed clothes, hot water, all the things like that. The only way to beat them is to tell lies.'

'But supposing you were found out?'

She laughed. 'You're a right eejit. There's thousands of us in the Forces. Thousands working in England. No one can check all the forms. It's the same with income tax. My father's working over here and claims against his tax for my granny and she's been in the Union for the last five years. He puts her down as living with us, that she's an invalid and needs special nourishment. Everyone does it, don't they?' She appealed to the other Irish girls. Each had a tale to tell, of defrauding the army or the inspector of taxes.

Thinking over the advice I had been given I knew I couldn't have lied on the form, whether from honesty or fear of being found out I was never sure. In the coming years, when I was promoted and earning more money, I made my mother a fairly generous allowance. But it never erased from her mind the years when all she got was half a crown, and many times she aired her grievance.

* * *

One evening, Deirdre and I were the only two in the barrack room. I'd been reading and had forgotten about her until she came to stand beside my bed. I saw that she was crying. She told me she had something to confess. 'It's something terrible,' she said. 'Promise you won't breathe a word of it.'

I surmised that she was pregnant. And the first thought in my mind was what happened to pregnant women in the army? Was it a serious crime? Surely to God the army wouldn't shoot you. Charge you, I supposed. Stop your pay. Send you back to Ireland. Back to Ireland and into the Union, for few parents would keep you at home. Into that terrifying building in James's Street. Where the inmates were dressed in rough grey clothes. Where men and women, even if married, were kept separate. That place, once the Foundling Hospital where un-wanted babies were placed in a basket, no questions asked, and passed through a hatch window, the majority to die in early infancy.

Poor Deirdre. My heart went out to her. 'Don't cry,' I told her, 'and talk easy in case anyone comes in.' I put an arm around her shoulders trying to hush her sobs. 'Hang on, I'll get down and we'll sit on the bottom bunk.'

'I'm a married woman,' she hiccuped through her sobs.

Thank God, I thought. That must have been the man on the boat. I asked her this and she glared with such hostility the crying stopped. 'What d'ye mean? What man? Wasn't I looking half the night for you.'

'I don't know what I'm saying. You gave me a terrible fright, you know, coming out with it so suddenly,' I lied. 'Go on, tell me. When did you get married?'

'Two years ago, and six weeks after he walked out on me and I never laid eyes on him since.'

'God that was a terrible thing. Did you search for him?'

'Everywhere. The morgue, the hospital, his relations, went to the police. He was a grown man, they said. They couldn't do anything about it. It was the slur. Being thrown over and everyone knowing it.'

I lit a cigarette and gave it to her. Then a drink of water and, remembering two squares of Tiffin bar I'd saved to eat in bed, gave her those as well.

'I knew they were all laughing behind my back in work. That's why I joined up. And another thing, I thought I might find him in England.' She finished the chocolate. 'I couldn't keep it to myself any longer. You're my best friend. But say as true as God you won't breathe a word of what I told you.'

I took an oath and a thought came into my mind.

'Maybe he could have lost his memory. I saw a picture about that.' It was the truth. I had seen such a picture and sincerely believed what I was telling her. 'This fella went out to work one morning. And didn't he slip and crack his head on the path.

Only a little bang. He didn't have to go to hospital. After a few minutes he got up and walked away. Only he couldn't remember who he was, his name, where he lived or worked, nothing, nor that he was married. He had money, after drawing out of his savings the day before for Christmas. But no papers, not even an envelope with his name and address. And wasn't he afraid to go to a hospital or the police. You know, like you could hear him talking to himself. "Maybe I'm a criminal. Like where did I get two hundred dollars? I'd best lie low. Get work. Any sort. And a room." And that's what he did. Moved to another town, got a room. Made up a name he'd seen over a shop. You saw his wife as well. She was gorgeous and broken-hearted like you. I was crying my heart out. Anyway he has this makey-up name and keeps moving from place to place. And then one day he's in Chicago or maybe San Francisco, I can't remember. It doesn't matter. He's waiting to cross the road when this little girl with lovely blonde hair lets go her mother's hand and runs out into the road. There's this big truck coming and doesn't your man run after her, pushes her out of the way but he's knocked down. Then you see him in hospital. And the doctors shaking their heads. He's been in a coma for weeks and they think he's going to die. And then he wakes up and his memory comes back. I was crying and laughing at the same time when I saw his wife and him together again. That could have happened to your husband.'

'Yeah, I suppose so,' said Deirdre with tears in her eyes. 'Maybe I shouldn't have joined up, for now he won't know where to find me.'

'Your mother'll tell him.'

'Yeah, you're right, so she will.'

The barrack room was filling up so we stopped talking but only after Deirdre had once again sworn me to secrecy.

Later in bed I thought about her story and again felt sorry for her. The shame and humiliation she would have suffered. She, like me, lived in a small community. People knew and helped each other. Lent each other shillings and sixpences. Shared cough bottles, passed on clothes that still had wear in them. Sat up with the dying, laid out the dead, delivered babies and knew everyone's business. As my mother used to say, 'They know what you have for breakfast.' And gossip of any kind added spice to their lives. Especially relationships between men and women. They'd divide into two camps. One supporting Deirdre. Branding her husband as a louser for deserting his wife. Wishing they could lay hands on him. Boasting of what they'd do to him. While the other camp would shake their heads and say, 'Ah well, it takes two to make a marriage. I wouldn't have wanted her for a daughter-in-law. And say what you like, he was a well-reared fella. Came from decent people.' And then some scandal from Deirdre's family would be recalled. Maybe a long-dead uncle, aunt, granny, or cousin at a long remove. 'That aunt of hers was flighty. Knocked around with British soldiers, even the Black and Tans and she a married woman. And as for her uncle he was a bowsie. Never sober a day in his life. And the granny would drink stout off of a sore leg. How d'ye know what that young man had to put up with?'

No wonder, I thought, Deirdre had run away. In the same circumstances so would I. And then another thought presented itself. Deirdre on the boat. Deirdre's habit of cadging. Deirdre the liar. Harmless lies so far. But lies all the same. And into my mind came a saying of my mother's: 'Give me a robber any day before a liar.'

I fell asleep convinced Deirdre had made up the story, as she did about the American soldiers, promoted to the rank of officers in her version, who had wanted another date with us. And how blatantly she had brushed aside my reference to the incident on the boat and pretended she had spent the night on board searching for me.

* * *

I was miserable. The weekend was approaching and Edith, Marj and the gang would be away on their seventy-two-hour pass. Bubbles too, off to Chester with her Yank. 'D'ye know what we could do?' the girl who had told me how to defraud the army and the income tax said to me at breakfast.

'What?'

'Apply for the seventy-two-hour pass, get a warrant and the ration money. Let on we're going away. Stay out all day. We'd have the money to buy meals. And sneak into barracks every night.'

Edith, who was sitting by us, pointed out it wasn't on.

'Why?' asked the Irish girl.

'This camp's too small. There's only one way in, through the main gate. The guard would spot you. Wait'll you're posted out. In a big mixed camp. Soldiers work the flanker all the time. Don't even bother to leave the camp. Eat their meals in the mess and pocket the ration money. But not here, cock. You'd be spotted in a minute and it's a serious charge.'

The Irish girl took her advice. But in years to come when stationed in a big camp I often worked the scam and only once was caught. But by that time I had learned the tricks of old soldiers and got away with it.

But now a long weekend was stretching in front of me without the company of my new dear friends. I decided to spend it concentrating on the following week when there were tests to sit that would decide what jobs we would be allocated.

Having scored the highest points at the intelligence tests on my first visit to Belfast, I felt confident of being able to pick and choose what I wanted to do. Physical training was top of my list; if that wasn't available then I'd be a driver. But it was the physical training I had set my heart on. Once I had left the training base never again would the uniform go on my back, unless at official parades. All day I'd trip round in shorts and track suits. And although we were forbidden to wear civilian clothes, I would risk it. Wear my lovely green and white check coat, civilian shoes and stockings. Everyone said, and I believed them, that away from the training barracks life was cushy.

SIX

On the Monday before the long weekend we were all in the cookhouse having our buns and cocoa and waiting for the post-corporal. There were no letters for me but one for each of the English girls, who on opening them each let out a whoop of joy then gathered in a huddle whispering to each other.

'Backbiting us,' said Deirdre, who with all her other faults had a suspicious mind. 'Not that I care. It's because we're Irish.' The huddle broke up and Edith came to where we sat. 'We didn't want to raise your hopes until our Mams wrote back. But it's OK. You can all come.'

'Come where?' I asked.

'Home with us for the weekend. You and Deirdre with me and we'll sort out the others.'

'You mean all of us. All the Irish girls?'

'Everyone who fancies it.'

Edith lived in Morecambe and so did Marj. Edith's mother and sister made us feel very welcome. We had a wonderful high tea on which her mother had spent some of her precious food points to buy Spam and tinned fruit.

Edith did imitations of the officers and Corporal Robinson's plummy voice and exaggerated the fools we'd made of ourselves when we had started drilling. All the stories were accompanied by hilarious actions, so that I thought I'd choke from laughing. Before the meal finished I felt as if I'd known the family all my life.

Edith's mother worked and had to leave when the meal was finished. She suggested that Deirdre and I should throw ourselves on the bed for half an hour before we got ready to meet up in the public house where she was a barmaid.

I'd noticed during tea that Deirdre was very quiet, although attempts were made to include her in all conversations. In the bedroom she started to cry. 'What ails you? Don't tell me you feel uncomfortable here. They're gorgeous people.'

'No, it's nothing like that.' She sniffed, blew her nose, wiped her eyes and said, 'I had a letter from my mother this morning. She's heard about Larry. That's my husband.'

'How did she find out? Where is he? Will you be able to go to him?'

'A fella from our street told her. He bumped into him in a public house in England.'

'That's great. So you will be able to find him.'

'I don't know about that. The fella didn't know much about him. Me ma only talked to him for a few minutes. He was over on embarkation leave and had just dropped in for a pint. He was going foreign the next day.'

'But he must have told your mother something?'

'He only mentioned a place called Lupinbeds, that's where he said Larry was.'

'That's a queer name for a town.'

'All the feckin' names in England are queer if you ask me.'

'Are you sure it was Lupinbeds?'

'Read the letter and see for yourself.' She found her mother's single sheet of ruled paper written in pencil and gave it to me. She was right about the place name—it was spelled out in block capitals.

Handing it back I said, 'Someone is bound to know where it is. Ask in the Company Office. Ask for an interview with the Junior Commander and tell her the whole story. She'll probably give you compassionate leave to look for him.'

'I can't,' she said, beginning to cry again, 'I joined up under a false name. Used my sister's birth certificate, she's still single. There's only ten months between us so no one could tell the difference.

'I joined up in my maiden name. God knows what the army'd do to me for false pretences. So you're never to mention anything I've told you.'

Knowing how all-powerful the army was, I didn't doubt that Deirdre would be in serious trouble for deceiving them. 'On my mother's life, not one word will ever pass my lips. So what'll you do?' I asked her.

'Once I leave the training centre I'll ask at railway stations anywhere I think that's safe and find out where Lupinbeds is. And I'll find him. I know that. I'll find him and get him back. After all, he is my husband. We were married in the sight of God.'

Deirdre's second confession had drained me. I felt like lying down and sleeping for a week. But soon Edith was at the door telling us to get a move on or there'd be no seats in the pub.

I got ready and coaxed Deirdre to do the same. I wore my fully fashioned khaki stockings not caring if I did bump into a military policewoman who would charge me for breaking King's Regulations. My courage boosted by Edith's reassurance that 'Where we're going, MPs don't,' I undid the bootlace from my hair. The ends were kinked, the laces having acted like curlers, and I wore a newly laundered collar. Newly laundered they chafed your neck but like fat women enduring the discomfort of tight corsets because they improved their appearance, I'd endure the collar.

To reach the public house we had to pass Morecambe Bay. The tide was in, the sun setting. A great expanse of water tinged red and gold stretched away towards Cumberland. In passing I noticed the beauty of the scene but my thoughts were more concerned with going to a public house for the first time and whether or not I would drink alcohol.

The bar was full of smoke, the ashtrays overflowing. There were a lot of men, mostly old. Old or not fit for call-up or in reserved occupations. Edith and Marj, who had joined us on the way with her Irish guests, were greeted rapturously: hugged and kissed, slapped on the back and bum. We were introduced. Drinks pressed on us. The room echoed with laughter. Everyone seemed to know everyone else.

'Aren't you going to drink that?' Deirdre asked, eyeing the glass of port wine I held.

'I'm not sure. What about my confirmation pledge?' I asked, forgetting about a previous drinking bout when I was sixteen.

'I broke mine ages ago. Give it to me if you don't want it.'

'I'll give it a try,' I replied, and sipped from the glass. I liked the taste and put to the back of my mind the day the Bishop confirmed me as a Christian and I promised never to let intoxicating drink pass my lips. I drank another two ports and lemon before leaving for a dancehall where Edith said there'd be lots of smashing fellas, soldiers and airmen, and never a red cap near the place.

The band played a selection of Glenn Miller, including 'In the Mood', to which Edith and Marj jitterbugged with amazing agility. They impressed the crowd so much that the floor was cleared for their exhibition. After a little while other couples took the floor, including Deirdre and a soldier. Her pinned-up hair had fallen round her shoulders, her cheeks—always rosy— were in full bloom and like a sponge ball she bobbed and bounced, kicked one leg from the knee then the other, leapt gracefully onto the soldier's hip. This was another side of Deirdre that I hadn't suspected existed.

For the first time in my life I wasn't a wallflower. Soldiers, airmen, young and not so young, danced with me. I was on cloud nine. I could have danced all night, the three glasses of port and two of cider (which I didn't think was alcoholic and which tasted delicious) relaxing my limbs, releasing my inhibitions and flooding my body with a wild sense of rhythm. You danced a dance, the band stopped. With your partner you waited for the music to begin again. Some of my partners slipped an arm round my waist while we waited for the band to start the next number. I didn't object to the intimacy. And lapped up the compliments. Sometimes after the third session of dancing my partner would ask, 'Let's have the next one,' as we walked off the floor. Sometimes they wouldn't. But immediately the band played again I was claimed. All too soon the band struck up the National Anthem and, remembering my English roots, I stood rigidly to attention.

Out in the cold air I felt decidedly queer but in the pleasantest manner. I was light-headed, light-footed. Floating along. Feeling as if any moment I could take off and fly. In my euphoric state nothing seemed beyond my capability. I sang and heard my voice soar loud and sweet and clear. I was drunk and not aware I was. We linked arms, Deirdre, Edith, Marj and the Irish girls. And from my schooldays a memory came to mind. The Palais Glide taught by a fat old nun as a number for a concert we were putting on. Then I'd had two left feet and brought Sister Bridget's unkind and personal criticisms upon me. 'Lord bless us,' I could hear her thick Kerry brogue, 'what sort of a pair of feet have you got at all?'

But tonight there was magic in the same feet, and singing 'There Were Ten Pretty Girls in the Village School' I glided with the grace of a swan until my head spun and I fell down, still holding on to Edith and Marj's arms, bringing them down on top of me. I felt the knee go out of one of my precious stockings and sobered immediately. Everyone else found the collapse hilarious and staggered about laughing. I cried for my stocking.

Edith's consolation didn't help. 'Buy another pair tomorrow, cock.'

'With what?' I asked.

'With the ration money.'

'But that's for your Mam for keeping me.'

She laughed derisively. 'Our Mam wouldn't take a penny from you. Our Mam's not like that.' And she wouldn't. Not only did she refuse the ration money but on the morning we left she gave me and Deirdre two shillings each—'for a few fags or sweets', she said, slipping us the florins.

Leaving I thanked her for the money, the hospitality and the gorgeous breakfasts. Bacon, eggs, the first real ones since I had left Dublin, and scallops which until then I had thought were luxury shellfish and which I had never tasted. Our Mam's were thick slices of potatoes fried to a golden crisp on the outside and inside as soft as butter. I promised that on my next leave in Ireland I'd buy her a present and send it to her. Meat, butter, clothes, anything that was scarce in England. Of course I never did. I never even wrote her a thank-you note, but after all these years I have never forgotten her kindness and generosity.

* * *

My visit to Bubbles' home in Liverpool the following week was completely different from the one to Morecambe. On Saturday night she said, 'Joe has to go to Liverpool tomorrow. Even if I could invite him to meet my parents he hasn't the time. I'll go along for the ride and surprise them. Would you like to come?'

I didn't need any persuading. Apart from going to Mass there was little to do on Sundays. Joe was outside the barrack gates in a jeep. Bubbles sat in the front. I was on an almost non-existent seat in the back. I kept thinking as we drove along, if only they could see me now in Dublin. In a jeep being driven by an American Air Force Officer. Joe was glamorous, the tallest man I had ever seen, blonde and handsome. Like a film star. He and Bubbles laughed a lot at jokes I didn't understand and in a

54

constant stream she passed me back Camels, chewing gum and Hershey Bars.

When we arrived in Liverpool she directed him to the suburb where she lived, where the houses were detached or semi-detached in streets with flowering trees, large gardens, and immaculate lawns. 'Next turn on the left and third house on the right,' said Bubbles.

'Pick you up on the corner at seven, hon,' Joe said before driving off. The house was detached, red-bricked and enormous. I followed her along the gravel-strewn drive and to the hall door with its panels of stained glass. 'Not a word,' she said before ringing the bell, 'about Joe, we hitchhiked, OK.' I nodded my acquiescence.

'Darling, what a lovely surprise,' a woman who looked like Bubbles said when the door opened. She smiled at me, stepped back and we went in. Then she and Bubbles exchanged kisses on each other's cheeks. From a room on the right-hand side of the hall a man appeared, a nice-looking elderly man who for a moment peered at us short-sightedly. 'And who is your friend?' asked her mother. At the same time Bubbles' father, who had come closer, exclaimed, 'Darling, we weren't expecting you.'

'Not disappointed,' she joked, then introduced me to her parents before kissing her father's cheek. Each parent in turn shook my hand, then her mother said, 'Let's go into the drawing-room. You must be thirsty. I'll make some tea.'

In their own way they made me as welcome as Edith's mother had. In their calm, polite, well-mannered way. But I didn't feel as immediately at home as I did at Morecambe. It was probably the voices, for I had been in houses as large and well furnished as theirs in Dublin. The house from which my grandmother had run away with an English soldier was twice as big and maybe a century older. So it had to be the voices and restraint of manner. Voices like the officers' and Corporal Robinson's. I had become used to how Bubbles spoke, and in any case her speech in barracks was laced with army jargon and the current slang.

Her father asked how we had got there. 'Hitchhiked,' she replied. 'Three lifts. A sweet old man and his wife, a doctor and a ride to the door in an American jeep.'

'Was that wise, darling?' asked her mother as she poured tea.

'I was a little apprehensive but it worked out fine. He was an officer with the American air force.'

55

'How will you get back, darling?'

Bubbles gave her father a dazzling smile. 'The same way, Dad, and you mustn't worry. Nowadays everyone hitchhikes.'

'I know dear, your father and I always stop for anyone in uniform. But when it's your daughter you can't help worrying,' her mother said before going to prepare lunch.

It was a generous and beautifully served meal. A tin of salmon—a precious item on points—and a salad of home-grown lettuce, tomatoes, spring onions and radishes. 'Dig for victory, I see,' said Bubbles as we sat down. The table was covered with an exquisitely drawn thread cloth, the china fine and matching and the cutlery gleamed. There was rhubarb tart for pudding with evaporated milk and, at the top of the dish, a dessert spoon and fork. Never having used a pudding fork before, I waited and watched to see how Bubbles did it.

During the meal her mother said, 'I had hoped there might have been a break during the course, one long enough for you to have got home.'

Bubbles shrugged. 'You know what the army's like. Keeps your nose to the grindstone.' Remembering my mother's penetrating eyes which seemed to bore into my brain, making a lie almost impossible to tell, and Bubbles' seventy-two-hour leave spent with her Yank in Blackpool, I marvelled at the unquestioning way her story was accepted. And wondered if voices were ever raised in this house.

Her parents tried very hard to make me feel at ease. They talked of holidays spent in Ireland before the war. How they enjoyed the salmon fishing. How welcoming everyone was. And told me when I was leaving that I must visit them again. They didn't slip me two shillings as Edith's mother had. I knew good manners, not lack of generosity, prevented them doing so. And I learned through the following years not to generalize about people. Not all northerners were outgoing, good-natured and generous. No more than all southerners were standoffish, cool, calm and collected. And that 'the voice' wasn't necessarily a guarantee of intelligence or education.

* * *

Every day after dinner Part Two orders were pinned to a notice-board in the corridor. It was obligatory to read them to discover your programme for the following days. Times of lectures, parades, inspections, interviews with officers and, on Monday after my visit to Liverpool, details of interviews which would lead to our job allocations. Mine was for two o'clock on the following day with Junior Commander Bulmer. After tea I got busy bulling my kit, and while pressing, spitting and polishing I planned what I would say. 'I'd like to be a Physical Training Instructress. And my second choice is to be a driver.' I saw myself tanned, in short shorts and a pale blue aertex shirt with a whistle swinging from my neck. Forming a class of girls into a circle, then with a sweep of my arm and in an encouraging friendly voice, clear but not too loud, calling, 'Running this way round, run.' Organizing games of netball. Teaching gentle rhythmic exercises. Correcting postures. All the things I had observed and learnt with such interest and pleasure.

Driving would be second best. I'd get to see lots of places in England. Wear the leather strap of my cap across its top. I never knew why drivers wore their caps so but it set them apart. Some drivers wore trousers. I longed for a pair of trousers.

The next day, smart as a new pin, I stood outside the office door nervous but hopeful that one of my choices would be granted. When given permission to enter I marched in, stood to attention and saluted. The officer was studying a file, leafing through it. She raised her head and told me to stand at ease, I moved one foot a shoulder's width from the other and clasped my hands behind my back. For a little while longer she perused the contents of the file before addressing me. 'Private Bolger,' she said, 'You're one of the difficult ones to place.'

'Yes ma'am.'

'Good IQ. Well above average but little education.'

'Yes ma'am,' I repeated like a parrot while I fumed inside. What did she mean? Little education? I'd been one of the best in my class. Best in English composition, history and geography. And I had the Primary Certificate of Education to prove it. And what about my elocution lessons? I had passed all the exams.

'Have you considered anything in particular you'd like to do?'

'I wanted to be a driver. But now I'd like to be a Physical Training Instructor.

'I see. Unfortunately they aren't chosen here unless that is what you were doing before joining up. After you're posted out you'll be observed and should you show an aptitude for physical training your instructor may suggest a course in the subject. However, that's all in the future. Driving is out, you've no mechanical aptitude.' Her voice droned on and on. 'With so little formal education I can't recommend you for signals nor clerical work.' My self-esteem fell through the floor and I longed to follow it. I was humiliated and angry, on the verge of crying. Regretting that I had ever joined up. Wishing I was back in the factory where everyone thought I was the most intelligent and best-educated girl in the place. Able to remember everything. Recite verse after verse of poetry. Use what they good-naturedly called 'jaw-breakers', words they didn't know the meaning of. And here I was being made little of. Told I was an ignoramus.

Through the open window came the sound of a squad marching, a drill instructor calling out commands. I wished I was out there with them. Wished I was anywhere but where I was.

'Have you considered cooking? You need intelligence for that. It's also a trade. For every examination passed you are upgraded and have a pay increment. And of course it fits you for civilian employment when you leave the forces.'

A civilian! My God, I had only just joined up and she was talking about when I finished.

'Are you listening, Private Bolger?'

'Yes ma'am.'

'Well, what do you think?'

'I suppose so, ma'am.'

I knew I'd hate it. I didn't join the army to be a cook. I kept the thoughts to myself. Outspokenness wasn't encouraged in the army.

'Well then, that's settled. I'll put your name forward for a course. You'll go to Aldershot. Quite a lively place. Magnificent avenue of chestnut trees along Queen's Avenue.' She gathered my papers and tidied them in the file. 'That's it then, you may go.'

I stepped back, saluted, about-turned and left the room.

On the way back to the barrack room I passed cooks leaving the mess hall, dressed in white stained overalls, their heads turbaned, black clogs on their feet. I was heartbroken to realize that for the rest of my service I was condemned to wear two of the most hideous outfits ever created.

I didn't moan or complain to the girls. And was surprised when they congratulated me on being chosen as cook.

'Smashing job, that,' Marj said. 'You have to have your buttons on to be a cook.' Edith pointed out all the perks that came the way of cooks. The pick of the food. Good money. Quick promotion. I let on to be pleased.

By tea-time we had all been allocated our jobs. Bubbles would do a driving course. An Irish girl who had worked in a hospital would be a medical orderly, and everyone else an orderly. For, like me, everyone else had no education.

I lay awake for hours, thinking about being a cook. Working all day in a roasting kitchen dressed in white overalls, black stockings and clogs. The smell of grease and fish always about you. Your face florid from the heat and growing fat from the pick of the food.

And then there was my mother. She'd go mad when she knew I was to be a cook. Increments, promotion, prospects of employment when I finished in the services. She'd dismiss all of those. I'd deserted her, given up a good job to become a skivvy. A drudge. I'd never hear the end of it.

I couldn't do it. I couldn't become a cook. I couldn't do that to her. But really it was the thought of the clogs, overalls and turban that made me go next morning, plead, cry and lie to the Junior Commander as to why I couldn't become a cook. Halfway to the office my courage almost failed me. Seldom had I ever stood up for what I thought was right. Not to teachers, nuns or employers. And here I was only five minutes in the army about to confront an officer. That most intimidating of beings. Deadpan faces, with the voice and power to stop your pay, confine you to barracks and God knew what else.

By the time I had reached the office I had worked myself into such a state of fear, resentment and dislike for the woman I believed had made little of me that I was crying when I entered the office.

The Junior Commander was so surprised she told me to sit down and asked, 'Why are you crying. Are you ill?'

'No ma'am,' I sobbed. 'It's just that I'm worried. I couldn't sleep last night. It's my mother. She mightn't let me come back when I go on leave if I'm a cook.'

'Do stop crying. I can hardly hear what you're saying. Your mother wouldn't let you come back from leave? Your mother would have no choice in the matter. Do control yourself and explain what you mean.'

'I'm from Ireland, from Dublin, ma'am. She was against me joining up and if she knows I'm a cook she'd stop me coming back. D'ye see, ma'am, you can't be touched by the British authorities in Southern Ireland.'

'I understand all about that,' she said, giving me a long steady look. While she did I noticed that her blonde hair was dyed. That she was really old. Forty maybe. Her eyes were a lovely colour, very pale blue. She could have been pretty once. But not now. She looked sick. Sick and tired. The flesh around her eyes was bruised and her skin had a yellowish tinge.

'Are you telling me you want to desert?'

'I wouldn't want to. Not desert, ma'am. I love the army. But you don't know my mother. And I'm in enough trouble over the allowance.'

'All the more reason to do the cookery course. Earn extra money and send it home.'

I surprised myself then by saying with tears, 'But I don't want to be a cook, ma'am.'

'Private Bolger,' she said with great control in her voice, 'you are being rather difficult. However, despite the limited choices available to you I'll see what I can do. You'll be informed in a day or two. And now you may go.'

'Thank you, ma'am.' I was off the chair, saluted smartly, about-turned and left the office in quick time, praying silently as I went that she would not summon me back to say she had changed her mind.

Two days later I was informed that I would be a switchboard operator. Marj and Edith thought I was bloody mad. Answering a telephone all day when I could have been a cook. Passing up all the perks cooks had. Daft as a brush I was, they concluded.

* * *

Hitler was dead. Mussolini was dead. Even in Ireland where the war scarcely touched us everyone had been aware of the two monsters. Forever and ever it seemed as if they would exist and with them so would the war. But they had met their ends and before I joined up the war in Europe had finished. Where or how I didn't know, not being one for reading newspapers or listening to news on the wireless and my mind already preoccupied with my decision to leave Ireland.

I did go into Dublin on VE night to witness how the peace was being celebrated. When the news of the Allied victory reached Dublin, Trinity College, an enclave of pro-British students, had run up the Union Jack. Nationalists then tied a Union Jack to Trinity's gates and set it on fire. The students responded by sending the Irish Tricolour up their flag pole flaming.

Riots followed. The windows of Trinity were showered in. So were those of the British Embassy and British shipping lines. Celebrating ex-servicemen, Irish veterans of World War One, gloriously drunk, raucously singing 'God Save the King', 'There'll Always Be an England', 'Rule Britannia', 'Roses in Picardy' and 'Tipperary', were dragged from side-cars and fights ensued.

In the ensuing melée I was tripped up and sprained my ankle. Even on that night you didn't have to wait hours in casualty. And I hobbled away from the Adelaide Hospital unintentionally sporting the English colours. A red and blue dress and a snowy white dressing round my ankle. No one paid me any attention.

No more than I paid to the Labour Party's overwhelming victory in the general election of 1945. Marj, Edith and almost all the English girls were ecstatic. In most of the public houses in the town, people were in jubilant mood. Free drinks were pressed on us from all sides. Deirdre accepted every one. I half carried her back to barracks and she cried all the way about her missing husband and how she would ever find Lupinbeds.

* * *

VJ Day. The War was really over. And again I wasn't aware of how or why. I don't remember anyone talking about Hiroshima or Nagasaki. All that concerned us was that we were having a day off to celebrate the final victory. A group of us decided to do our celebrating in Chester, hitchhiking there in an American jeep. Laughing and singing. Smoking Camels, chewing gum. Not noticing when I did arrive that Chester was a beautiful town. Aware only of the joyous atmosphere of strangers greeting strangers like long-lost relatives. Dancing, kissing, embracing. Music, singing. Couples clicking. The kissing becoming more passionate. The embraces less discreet. No one fell over themselves to grab me or Deirdre. All the same I enjoyed myself. Carried along on the wave of joy, laughing, singing and dancing in the street.

* * *

Our six weeks' training was almost over. Tomorrow we would know our postings. Soon we would be gone. Another contingent of rookies sleeping in our bunks. Never before had we made such close friendships with strangers. Poured out our hopes and secrets to girls who six weeks previously we didn't know existed. Advised each other, laughed and cried together. Shared all we had. A coming together we would remember all our lives and never experience again.

The postings were up. Lancashire and Cheshire girls who had asked to be sent to the north-west were allocated to camps in East Anglia and the Home Counties. Irish girls who'd requested London, Birmingham and Coventry were sent to Wales and Devon. Deirdre was going to Catterick Camp, and instead of Brighton I was going to the Isle of Man.

'Told you, didn't I,' Edith said after reading the list of postings. 'Ask for Scotland and you'll get Cornwall. But you'll like the Isle of Man, Pad. Smashing place that. We used to go there on day-trips before the war.' Deirdre was considered the luckiest. Those in the know said Catterick Camp was chock-a-block with men. She whispered to me, 'I wonder if it's anywhere near Lupinbeds.'

* * *

Without being aware of it, we had been brainwashed. Corporal Robinson had imbued us with *esprit de corps*. We wanted to be the winning squad on the Passing-Out Parade, and during the run-up to it we worked like Trojans. Marched perfectly. Kept our arms straight. Swung them shoulder-high. Wheeled, marked time on the spot, left-turned, right-turned, about-turned as if our movements had been choreographed.

The night before leaving we copied down each other's new camp addresses. Promised never to lose touch and once every two years to have a reunion.

We weren't the winning squad. Nevertheless, Corporal Robinson congratulated us on putting on a good show. Hoped we'd continue to be a credit to the army and wished us luck.

There were no tears on the morning of our leaving. They'd been shed the night before in the pub and before we went to bed. Now we were nervous and excited at the prospect of new places, new adventures. Deirdre got me alone and extracted a promise to enquire about Lupinbeds, to write every week and meet in Dublin on our first leave. And then I was on my way. Carrying my battered suitcase and long khaki kitbag. Staggering along the railway platform to find the Regimental Transport Officer for my travelling instructions to Fleetwood, where I would board the Isle of Man steamer. Where eventually I sat amongst strangers, apprehensive, heading for a place I knew nothing about except that the cats were reputed to have no tails. Dreading my arrival. A new girl having to make herself known. Learning to work a switchboard, something I'd never laid eyes on before.

SEVEN

The sea was calm and the day sunny. I sat on deck eating the bully-beef sandwiches provided as rations and thought about my friends travelling to different parts of the country. Bubbles off to her driving course. Marj, Edith and the rest to be orderlies wearing khaki overalls and matching turbans. Serving food, wiping down tables. Deirdre, who despite her cadging and moaning I'd miss. I wondered if Bubbles would find an old, loaded brigadier or become a GI bride.

As soon as I was settled in I'd write. I watched the seagulls following the boat, soaring, for minutes remaining motionless in the sky, calling in their complaining voices. Land came into sight, then buildings. We were nearly in. A strange place. Me, a stranger, having to make myself known. Not at all like basic training, where we were all strangers. Anxiety beset me. Supposing I couldn't learn how to operate a switchboard? What would happen to me then?

The boat docked. A truck was waiting to take me to my billet, which turned out to be a very grand hotel on the Front. I reported to an ATS sergeant who ticked my name off on her millboard, and told me I would work a shift system in a hotel called the Villiers close by. She had a private show me my sleeping quarters and told me a meal would be provided if, after depositing my kit, I went to the cookhouse.

My hotel bedroom overlooked the sea. The private who brought me to it was Scottish and I took a liking to her. We introduced ourselves. Her name was Morag. 'This is a cushy number and the grub is great. You'll like it here. Everyone does,' she said.

It was a double room furnished with four single beds. The

floor was carpeted, and there was plenty of cupboard space and a wash basin. Yes, I thought, I will like it here.

Morag left and two other girls arrived and greeted me with great friendliness. They were clerks in the Company Office and English. Without 'the voice', well spoken. Their accents I couldn't recognize. Pointing to a barracked bed, they told me it was mine and the one in the corner next to it was Barbara's.

'She's the telephonist you'll be working with,' one said. I noticed that only my bed was barracked and asked why the other three weren't.

The second girl explained you only barracked in training centre, for inspections or when, like mine, the bed was waiting for a new occupant. 'You can make yours up now.' She helped me. I relaxed.

I'd get along with these girls.

* * *

After dinner I went to meet Barbara in the small telephone exchange. She was the prettiest, most glamorous girl I had ever seen. Everything about her was perfect, gorgeous. Black wavy hair, big, dark-lashed blue eyes. Teeth like an advertisement for toothpaste and even in her khaki skirt and shirt her figure was fabulous. Big bust and tiny waist.

As soon as she spoke I recognized her accent—she was from Northern Ireland. And of course she could tell I was from Dublin.

We talked for a little while. Telling each other where we came from in our respective cities. How long we had been in the Forces. And all the time I was mesmerized by her beauty. The smile which lit her face. By comparison I felt so unattractive with my naked face and hair wound round a bootlace from which lank strands had escaped. But I was not jealous, for she exuded warmth, charm and friendliness.

'Well, I suppose I'd better show you the ropes.' She sat in front of the little switchboard and told me to bring a chair and sit beside her.

'Just watch what I do, it's dead easy.'

It wasn't a very big board. Maybe eighteen inches to two feet square and fixed to a bench. Its face was covered with numbered metal discs and beneath each number was a hole. At the bottom of its face there was a double row of metal prongs and to the side of the board a handle protruded.

Barbara explained: 'It's what's called a doll's-eye board. If someone rings the exchange a metal eyelid drops on the number and clicks up and down until the call is answered. Then you pick up one of these,' she demonstrated, catching hold of a metal prong and pulling it out. To it was attached a lead. 'Stick this in the hole beneath the clicking eyelid and push this forward.' She pointed out a double row of switches in front of the panel of prongs. 'And Bob's your uncle.'

She looked at her watch and I noticed her long filbert-shaped nails painted a brilliant red. 'Everyone's still in the mess or cookhouse. But after two you'll see me in action.'

She gave me more information. 'You never leave the board unattended until six o'clock. After six a line is transferred to the guardroom in case of an emergency.' She showed me printed lists of the board's numbers with the rank and designation of the man or office whose number it was.

'And these, the ones underlined in red, are the "sir or ma'am" numbers. No matter how many eyelids are clicking these get priority. You'll pick it up as you go along. And never forget the Colonel gets top priority. He's an oul' bollocks. Thinks he's God. Like a lot of peacetime soldiers he hasn't got used to the idea of women in the Forces. Army Tool-Softeners, that's what some of them call us. Not to our face, mind you. D'ye know something, you don't hear much swearing. Not like Dublin or Belfast, where a lot of fellas think nothing of saying "fuck" in front of a woman.'

She showed me telephone directories and how to call the civilian operator. She rambled on. So much information I thought my head would burst. Now and then she stopped and said, 'Don't worry, kid, it'll all fall into place.'

Before two o'clock she repaired her face. Reapplied her lip-stick and dabbed round her nose and cheeks with a powder puff, all the time scrutinizing her features in a compact mirror.

On the stroke of two o'clock, doll's eyes closed and clicked up and down. I watched and listened. Noticing that when it was a 'sir' or 'madam' call Barbara's Belfast accent became a fair imi-tation of 'the voice'. 'Number, please. Yes, sir. Yes, ma'am. Trying to connect you. Sorry to keep you waiting. I'm sorry, there's no reply. Shall I call you back? You're through now.

Hold the line, please.'

I listened and tried to memorize. I also listened when the call wasn't from a sir or ma'am. When it was someone Barbara was familiar with. When she laughed and made double-meaning remarks. Arranged to see some of the callers sometime. I pondered the meaning of 'Army Tool-Softener'. I'd never heard the phrase before. Knowing that 'tool' was one of the many euphemisms for a man's penis, I thought it must have something to do with sex. But what?

I knew so little about sex. One night when I'd been in a friend's house plastering bread with condensed milk, some of the thick, white sticky liquid spilled down the front of my dark brown coat. My mother threatened to kill me when I came home. She shook and slapped me while demanding an explanation which she didn't allow me to give. My brother and sister looked on, terrified and unable to say a word in my defence.

'It's only condensed milk,' I managed to say. 'Look.' I wet my fingers, rubbed at the stain and sucked them. I was so innocent or ignorant that it was years before I realized what she had suspected. The row blew over as they always did and we sat down to supper as if it had never taken place.

About an hour after my tuition began, Barbara suggested I have a go. I put on the headpiece and apprehensively answered a few uncomplicated calls. Barbara congratulated me and I felt a surge of confidence. 'Listen,' she said, 'I want to slip out. I won't be a minute. I have to see this fella in the stores. Will you be alright?'

'I think so, but don't be long.'

'Only a tick,' she promised, and left. A few lids dropped and I coped, congratulating myself on my competence. Then another call came through and a voice asked for the divorce sergeant. Remembering one of Barbara's pat phrases I stalled. 'Hold the line. I'm trying to connect you,' I said as I frantically scanned a list looking for the number of a divorce sergeant. 'Sorry to keep you waiting,' I remembered to say as panic almost choked me. The earpiece became clammy with sweat and still no listing of a divorce sergeant. Then as if my guardian angel had alighted on my shoulder and whispered the question in my ear I repeated it. 'I didn't hear you properly, could you repeat the number, please.'

Back came the answer in a resigned tone, 'The provost

sergeant.' I made the connection and heaved a sigh of relief, telling myself it was all a matter of common sense. All the same I wished Barbara would hurry up. Then my guardian angel deserted me, went for a fag, a pee or whatever guardian angels do when not perched on your shoulder. And down came the Colonel's shutter, clicking like a demented grasshopper. I plugged in. 'Number please, sir.' A voice barked, 'Get me Manobier.'

'Yes, sir. Hold the line.'

I talked to myself. Jesus, Mary and Joseph, where is Manobier? India. I'd heard the name. Heard it in a picture. A place in India. Like Bombay, Bengal, Calcutta. How would I get through to India? Deception aided me. I plugged into a hole without a number and turned the handle. After a suitable interval I said, 'I'm sorry, sir, there's no reply, shall I call you back?'

'Keep trying and call me immediately you get it,' he snapped. Click, click, the eyelid danced up and down. Please God, help me, I prayed as I picked up and pushed in the pronged lead. At one and the same time two things happened. Barbara came in the door and the Colonel barked, 'Cancel my call to Manobier.'

I pulled off the headset, put my head in my hands and cried. Barbara was full of concern. Asking what ailed me. What had happened. I ignored her, stood up and ran through the door.

Sitting on the lavatory, the fright abated, anger taking its place. Anger at myself for not being able to cope, with Barbara for staying away so long. Gradually I calmed down and began telling myself how I should have handled the Colonel. Politely I should have said, 'This is my first day, sir. I don't know where Manobier is or how to connect you.' With hindsight how easy it seemed. But the Colonel's voice had intimidated me. My mother could have done it. No man or woman, whatever their position or voice, would have overawed my mother.

I blew my nose, dried my eyes and to cool my face wetted a wad of toilet-paper stamped WD, War Department, hard enough, as Edith used to say, 'to reef the arse of you'.

Barbara laughed hysterically when I told her of the incident. 'India,' she cackled. 'What gave you that idea? Manobier's in Wales. There, look.' She held out the list. And there it was. Anti-Aircraft School of Artillery, Manobier.

* * *

Life on the Isle of Man was pleasant and relaxed. You seldom saw an officer except on pay parade. Occasionally we drilled on the promenade, occasionally we had a lecture to attend. At one, given by a young doctor on health matters, a question was asked from the floor. Was smoking bad for your lungs? Confidently and emphatically the young doctor explained that at post-mortem the lungs of a city dweller whether he smoked or not were dark and the lungs of a man who had spent his life in the country irrespective of his smoking habits a healthy pink.

* * *

In no time I mastered the switchboard and enjoyed my four-and-a-half-hour shifts. In between calls I read, wrote letters and gossiped with people who dropped in.

The town was only around the corner from the hotel. There were shops, cinemas and cafés where I sat drinking tea and making dates. Sometimes three for the same night, staggering the times in case one or the other didn't turn up. Sometimes they didn't but seldom did all three let you down.

I learned how to kiss and how to ward off the advances almost every soldier attempted. Frequently I took a chance and wore civilian clothes though they were still forbidden. My green tweed coat was greatly admired and often borrowed, so much so that one date said, 'Pad, it's a smashing coat—who owns it?'

'Me,' I said. I don't think he believed me.

Life was wonderful. So little work. So much leisure. So many dates.

Remembering the factory sometimes—the dirt, dust, noisy machines, the rats in the cellar, the filthy room where our tea was made, the vile lavatories—I congratulated myself on the change I'd made.

It was good to be alive and young. To have friends, good quarters, nice food and dates and dates and dates. And there were the German POWs who were interned on Douglas. Not all blonde giants, but almost all attractive—their foreignness enhancing their appearance.

Life was good except when my mother's letters arrived. She never failed to remind me that I had left her with half a crown a week and that she hoped God would forgive me for what I had done.

So I requested an interview with my Junior Commander. She was a sweet-faced woman. Invited me to sit down and listened as I explained about the dependant's allowance and asked was there any way in which I could earn extra money. Truthfully I didn't at this stage care whether I could or couldn't. But at least I could write and tell my mother I hadn't forgotten that I had left her short of money.

The JC was sympathetic. I told her of my ambition to be a PTI. And she explained how there wasn't one on the island.

'They, as you already know, are the ones who do the talent-spotting. You could try a course of shorthand and typing. There are courses here. A successful course could get you a clerical job and more money. What d'ye say?'

I knew the courses were held in the evenings. I liked my evenings free. Going to the pictures with my date, sitting in the cafés, walking along the Promenade and snogging.

But she was so kind, so understanding, I didn't have the heart to refuse. 'I'll try it, ma'am,' I said and prepared to leave. Before I could salute she said, 'Let me show you something,' and beckoned me to the window. 'There,' she said, pointing to the sea. 'Over there is the coastline of Ireland. I expect sometimes you feel homesick. Then it would be good to look at the sea and assure yourself that you're not too far away from home.'

'Thank you, ma'am.' I didn't disillusion her. Didn't tell her that since the one night in Training Centre when homesickness had overwhelmed me I rarely gave Dublin or Ireland a thought.

* * *

I hated the typing course. My fingers, so nimble with a needle, performed like thick pork sausages. And the shorthand made no sense at all. I felt stupid and awkward and like many fools looked for something to laugh at. Someone or something to blame for my failure. The instructor. It was her fault. She was too old. She wore thick sugar-bag blue knickers that I knew would have a fleecy lining. My mother and all old people wore them in the winter. The knickers were worn pulled over her stocking tops so that when she bent to demonstrate or remonstrate you could see them. I laughed to myself each time I witnessed the spectacle. It consoled me for my ineptitude. She was a patient, kindly woman who encouraged me, assuring me that eventually I'd master the typing if not the shorthand. That typing was a worthwhile skill. I should persevere. And I promised I'd try harder although I had already decided to leave the course.

* * *

Barbara was easygoing and pleasant to work with. I wasn't the best timekeeper but she never complained when I was late relieving her. But as time passed she became more inquisitive as to how I got on with the fellas I dated. Asking such questions as how far did I let them go. This surprised and embarrassed me.

I'd hem and haw and change the subject. Apart from embarrassment I didn't want to admit to Barbara that at the first feel of a hand descending anywhere on my thick tweed coat or layers of blanket-cloth khaki below my waist, back, front or in the region of my chest, I disengaged myself and left my date without explanation. If I confessed this to Barbara she'd think me a thick, and holy into the bargain.

One day she sat pushing back her cuticles with an orange stick and out of the blue announced, 'I'm what you might call a "technical virgin".'

'Are you? That's great,' I said, as if technical virginity was as familiar to me as answering the switchboard.

'It's the only way. Let them go as far as possible, almost the whole hog but not quite.'

I was avid with curiosity. About technical virgins, how and what was as far as possible. So much I wanted to know. Why were some soldiers and girls called Geordies, Brummies, Scousers? How could you tell a sergeant from a staff-sergeant, a first lieutenant from second lieutenant, a colonel from a major? But I knew all these puzzles would be solved in time. They would have already been solved had I paid more attention during lectures. But who could I ask about technical virgins? Certainly not Barbara. For all that she was beautiful and pleasant, there was something about her that made me feel uneasy. I think it was her smile. She conjured in my mind pictures of beautiful witches in fairy tales. The bad fairy in 'Sleeping Beauty'. The Queen in 'Snow White'. A smiling figure who beckoned. My vivid imagination? But that's the feeling she gave me—someone who would lead me astray.

Next time I wrote to Edith I'd ask her about technical virgins. She was bound to know. Edith knew everything.

Then one day in the middle of her probing questions and my attempt to parry them she suddenly changed the subject. 'I forgot to tell you there's a rumour going round that we're being disbanded.'

'Oh, no. But why?' I asked.

Barbara shrugged. 'I suppose because the war's over. Lots of units will be disbanded. I wonder where we'll be posted?'

I was posted to Catterick Camp, Barbara to Fort William. I never saw or heard of her again.

EIGHT

Deirdre was stationed in Catterick but a week before I left the Isle of Man she sent a card. She was moving to somewhere in Kent. Later on she'd send her new address.

I liked the girls I had met in Douglas but there wasn't a great sadness when I left them. Not the pain of parting I had experienced at Training Centre. Barbara winked and advised me not to do anything she wouldn't do, adding, 'and that gives you a lot of scope'.

There was a gale blowing as the steamer left Fleetwood, reminding me of the night Deirdre and I had sailed to England. I never thought I'd miss her. In fact I hadn't. All the same it was comforting to think she might be still at Catterick Camp when I arrived. She hadn't mentioned her lost husband since I had seen her last. And I wondered had she found out where Lupinbeds was.

I wondered so many things about her. Every Sunday morning she and I had gone to Mass and received Communion. I'd watch her walk devoutly back to her seat and kneel with bowed head and I'd wonder had she confessed the sin she had committed on the boat. How would she get the nerve? And if she didn't how could she receive Communion? That would be a sacrilege for which, should she die suddenly, she would go straight to Hell.

I shuddered, not sure if it was the horrendous thought of roasting in Hell or the stiff breeze blowing off the sea. More than likely it was the breeze. For lately I thought less and less about death, dying and Hell. Since joining up I had not seen a funeral nor heard of anyone dying. Not even of anyone being sick.

In Ireland all of that was part of daily life. Death, religion, sin. Novenas, miraculous medals, indulgences granted for so

73

many prayers said for the dead in Purgatory. Indulgences you could gain while still alive to reduce your sentence when you died. Young and old men and women belonging to lay religious orders who had already purchased their habits.

In reality it wasn't as macabre as it sounds. For girls could switch from describing the shade of blue shroud to the colour of the outfit they were wearing for Easter or Whitsun. And my mother talked about her burial policies and grave receipt with less emotion than her wad of pawn tickets.

While pondering these thoughts I was devouring my ration sandwiches, which were meant to last me to Catterick, when a pleasant voice in a gorgeous foreign accent put a stop to my mind's meanderings. He was a Polish soldier, blonde, green-eyed and handsome. He told me his name was Zladimir but that in England everyone called him George.

'Why?' I asked.

He smiled, displaying wonderful, big, strong white teeth. 'They tell me Zladimir is not easy to, to,' he paused searching for a word.

'Pronounce,' I suggested.

'Ah, yes, pronounce, that is it. So, I am George.'

I told him my official Christian name.

'Helena. A beautiful name. In Poland there are many Helenas.'

'At home I'm called Nellie. I hate that. It's an old woman's name.'

'Change it. Be Nell or Nella. If you were Jewish that's what you'd be, Nella, that's pretty.'

He bought me a cup of what was sold on board as coffee. It was no worse than the NAFFI brew. I drank it and we continued talking. We discovered we were both going to Catterick. We swapped our camp addresses and when we were about to dock he went to find his mates, promising that he'd see me on the train.

I looked for him when we disembarked at Fleetwood but didn't see him. The train to Crewe was jammed with servicemen and women carrying cumbersome kitbags, haversacks, rolled-up groundsheets, tin helmets, the men's tunics criss-crossed with khaki webbing from which tin mugs and mess tins were suspended. They packed the carriages six to a seat. I was squashed between two soldiers. Those without seats jammed the corridors in such numbers that it was impossible to go to the lavatory or look for Zladimir.

It was 'all change at Crewe'. The train emptied. There was a two-hour wait for my connection and a stampede into the waiting-room. I had a cup of tea then felt I would suffocate and went outside where, despite my thick uniform and double-breasted greatcoat, the cold was biting. My feet began to stagnate. To keep the circulation going I walked up and down the platform having left my baggage outside the waiting-room, not caring if someone did steal it, not considering how, if it was stolen, I'd be charged with being careless and have to pay for all items of missing army property. Back and fore, back and fore I walked, now regretting my hasty exit from the waiting-room, aware that it was a hope of finding the Polish soldier rather than lack of air that had sent me rushing out.

In those days waiting-rooms had coal fires, a woman attendant and long benches where weary travellers with a long wait, sometimes an all-night one, could stretch out and sleep.

When my train did arrive I was already poised, ready to push, shove and fight my way on board and secure a seat. Which I did, one by a window.

Everyone was squashed against someone else. Everyone was smoking. Everyone tired and probably hungry. Yet the atmosphere wasn't only filled with smoke. There was also good humour in the air. There were three other girls besides me. Some of the soldiers flirted clumsily but amusingly. No one swore offensively, no double-meaning remarks were made. Anyone with rations left offered them around. One RASC private generously divided a bar of chocolate between the girls.

Now and then the train thundered through stations, passed towns where lights were strung out and foundries sent up plumes of smoke and flares of flames. We dozed and woke at stations where the train drew to a juddering halt and sleepy voices asked, 'Where are we?' Sometimes it was where they were supposed to be and frantically they scrambled out.

Before I arrived at my destination few passengers were left and so it was possible to reach the lavatory, only to be almost asphyxiated by the stench of male urine when I opened the door. Of Zladimir I saw no sign. He had made an impression on me. I couldn't understand how we had missed each other, but consoled myself that at Richmond Station I was bound to see him. And if I didn't, we were going to the same camp and we'd bump into each other sometime.

Little did I know how vast Catterick Camp was. Little did I know how cold the wind would be when I stepped out onto the platform at Richmond. It knifed through my many layers of clothing.

There was a truck to take me to the guardroom where the duty ATS NCO was waiting for my arrival. From the guardroom I was delivered to the cookhouse for a meal of grey, greasy stew and tea. Tea that tasted almost as good as what we drank at home. I later learned it was called sergeant-major's tea. The tea of cooks, duty warrant officers and non-commissioned on their rounds during the night. It hadn't stewed for hours in vast urns, washing soda hadn't enhanced its strength or flavour. Perhaps the rumoured bromide wasn't added. Perhaps sergeant-majors didn't need, or weren't to have, their libidos damped down. In any case the tea was delicious. Warm, comforting and invigorating. I had a new lease of life. Forgot the long, uncomfortable train journey, the cold, my disappointment at not meeting my Polish soldier. Catterick Camp might be a great place. I remembered how in Training Centre it had been said there were thousands of blokes there. I could be in for a marvellous time.

But I was quickly disillusioned when the truck that had brought me to the guardroom transported me to my billet. The duty NCO accompanied me. Warning me on the way not to make any noise as the girls who shared the billet were mess orderlies and had to be up at six o'clock the following morning. 'There's a light left on in the passage and on the landing. You'll find your way about. Tomorrow report to Cambrai Lines at nine o'clock. To the guardroom. The telephone exchange is there.'

The billet was an ex-married quarter, a two up and two down with a scullery and outside lavatory. A low-watt bulb burned in the hall. The house was freezing. I went up the stairs on tip-toe. Looked into both small bedrooms. Saw one with a barracked bed. Unpacking only my pyjamas I made the bed up. Stiff with cold, aching with fatigue and tense for fear of waking the sleeping occupants, I crept awkwardly about my task.

When I got between the sheets they felt as if they had been drenched with icy water. Sleep was impossible. I got up, put on my vest and knickers and my stockings under my pyjamas, jammed the pyjama legs into the stockings and knotted their tops to keep them up. But still I was shivering. Out of bed again, this time to find my pullover. Over the pyjamas it went. I wrapped a khaki woollen scarf around my head, threw my greatcoat across the bed, got in and eventually shivered myself to sleep.

When I woke the next morning the little house was empty. My breath was visible in the icy room. I had never felt so forlorn and miserable in my life. I thought with longing of the Training Centre and my hotel bedroom on the Isle of Man. Then a glance at the clock sent me into a fearful frenzy. I had slept it out, missed my breakfast and if I didn't hurry would be late reporting to the telephone exchange. A quick glance round the room showed me that the other beds were made up. So I plumped my pillows, smoothed and tucked in the brown army blanket which was its covering. Had a cat's lick, as a perfunctory wash is called in Ireland, kicked my kitbag and case out of sight, ran a comb through my hair, went outside and asked a passing soldier the way to Cambrai Lines. Huddled in his greatcoat, not stopping, he called instructions as to how to get there.

It was a long walk. Everywhere in Catterick Camp, I was to discover, was a long walk from everywhere else. It was a great sprawl of a place, bleak and seemingly always scoured by biting winds. Individual camps within the main sprawl were designated as Lines and named after First World War battle sites.

The guardroom was a single-storey building. Whitewashed boulders lined the concrete path and on a concrete square set in the grass stood a brass cannon. Off the main guardroom, manned by regimental police, was the telephone exchange, identical to the one on the Isle of Man. There was a pot-bellied cast-iron coke-burning stove, with which I was delighted, though later I discovered its fumes gave me headaches.

From time to time during my shift a regimental policeman would put his head round the door and ask if I was OK. I saw through the window a bucket of tea being delivered. Sergeant-major's tea. I was included in the share-out. By the time my relief took over I knew the names of all the men and they called me Paddy.

My relief's name was Ruby. She came from Walthamstow. She arrived half an hour early and we chatted. Her hair was tightly permed, the black of a dead crow, grey roots along her parting. Her lipstick was a vivid red, thickly applied, and orangey pancake make-up emphasized lines round her mouth.

She admitted to being thirty-five. During our chatting I asked her what she thought of Catterick. 'Not much.'

'There's supposed to be lots of blokes, so I was told.'

'Yeah,' she said, 'and every one of them after the same thing. Randy buggers. But it's the Poles you want to watch. Bite your nipples off they do.'

My hand went to my breast pocket. 'Honest to God?'

'On my mother's life. Ask anyone who's been out with a Pole.'

In my mind's eye I saw Zladimir's handsome face and thought, surely not him. He wouldn't do a thing like that. Then I remembered his big, white gleaming teeth. All the better to bite me with. Not, of course, I told myself, that I'd ever let a man's hand never mind his teeth near my breast. A girl who did was asking for trouble even if she didn't lose her nipples. During the following years I dated men of many nationalities but never a Pole. So I can't comment on their foreplay.

Ruby was married. Her man was with Thirty Corp stationed in Germany. She had a solid-gold watch and several rings set with diamonds and other precious stones. She told me they were valuable and brought in to show me a beautiful silver bowl with delicate engravings round its sides, and when she lifted the lid a big downy puff smelling of powder rose slowly. 'All', she said, 'for a few fags and a packet of coffee.'

I didn't understand. She explained. 'For fags and coffee you can get anything in Germany, even a woman. Cars as well, though I expect you would have to give a load of fags for a car. Fred's brought me home jewellery, silver cutlery, all sorts of things. See, the Germans are starving. They'd give anything for a bit of food and tobacco.'

* * *

In Catterick I felt lonely and miserable. The mess orderlies with whom I shared the house were, when I came off duty, either sleeping, out or at work. And the personnel from my unit were scattered over the camp so that I only glimpsed them once a week on pay parade. And as for dates I had none. Some of the men from the guardroom chatted me up and asked me out, but I didn't fancy any of them. They were mostly ancient and, I suspected, married.

For the first time since leaving Ireland I began to feel unwell. Vague aches and pains. Listless and feverish. When I mentioned this to Ruby she said I should report sick. Then added, 'The MO'll probably say you're malingering. Not out straight, though. But all you'll get is medicine and duty.'

I wasn't familiar with the word malingering and asked what it meant and what was medicine and duty. 'That he doesn't believe there's anything wrong with you. So he'll give you a bottle, probably chalk or coloured water and a number nine which'll run the guts out of you. All the same, you don't look right so go sick in the morning.'

I did and was admitted to the garrison hospital. I never knew what ailed me but enjoyed being tucked up in bed in a centrally heated ward, fed well, given dozens of M&B tablets, a sulphonamide drug, the forerunner of penicillin. I hoped for a long stay in hospital. But after ten days I was discharged and out I went into the cold. Airy-headed and on hollow legs I made my way to the Company Office to report 'fit for duty', and to my delight discovered that my unit was soon to be posted to the South of England. I made a miraculous recovery.

The South of England. Brighton, where my father had gone to school. Where a sister of his still lived. The one who'd been educated at the Sacred Heart Convent in Roehampton. Horsham, the home of my grandfather. I'd visit him and my aunt. Meet the Ravishing Lancer with whom my grandmother had eloped. She'd been disowned by her father for marrying an English soldier and, worse still, a Protestant.

He'd tell me about her. My grandmother, Fanny, my second Christian name. He'd talk about my father. Describe him as a boy. A young man. It would be like bringing him to life again.

NINE

The regimental band played 'Waltzing Matilda', the 'Royal Artillery Inspection March' and a selection of popular melodies. Officers and NCOs marched up and down the platform clutching boards, studying lists, calling orders, checking the occupants of carriages.

The three of us – myself, a sweet-faced girl from Ireland whose name was Breda and a Scottish girl called Katy, girls who were from my unit but whom I'd only met since boarding the train – hung out of the window watching the activity. Exhilarated by the music, the prospect of a new posting. New places, new faces. Gradually the platform cleared. A guard walked along it checking the compartment doors. The massive engine belched steam. The guard blew his whistle. And the train began its journey south, taking me to some of the happiest years of my life.

Breda was from rural Ireland. Apart from her eyes, which were big and grey with a beautiful gentle expression, I thought her nondescript, totally unlike Katy, who was vivacious, quick-tongued and wore the smartest uniform I had ever seen—her collar stiffly starched, knife-like creases in her skirt, and her cap at a rakish angle around which her hair curled in wisps. Her teeth were brilliant, like an American's, in her wide, white smile.

From time to time as we went south soldiers opened the carriage door asking for lights, making small talk. With smart answers and crushing wit Katy sent the unacceptable ones packing.

We ate our rations. Bully beef and Spam sandwiches, sausage rolls in a leaden pastry and minute bars of chocolate. We smoked and talked.

The hours sped by.

The lights were on again all over the world. London was lit

up. We transferred to a coach that would take us to Waterloo Station. I saw Big Ben and the Houses of Parliament, thrilled to be seeing sights only seen before in books and films. I felt as if I knew them from all the times my father had talked about London. All the times he had promised he would one day take me there. And for a brief moment I wished he was alive so that I could write and tell him I had seen them.

From Waterloo we went to a station called Brookwood in Surrey, and from there to an army camp on the border of Surrey and Hampshire. It was long past midnight when we arrived so it was difficult to get an impression of the camp. But the air was soft, smelled wonderful; there was a light breeze, so unlike the knifing winds that blew in Catterick.

The billets were spider huts, wooden structures with a central body where store rooms, ablutions and the central heating were located. Three supposed spider's legs protruded on each side of the body, in each of which was our sleeping quarters. There was a gorgeous smell of wood. And as we were into October, the month in which the heating was switched on, the atmosphere was welcoming.

Breda, Katy and I chose beds next to one another, dumped our kit and, as ordered on arrival, assembled outside. By torchlight, an NCO led us down a steep incline to the cookhouse where a passable meal was laid on. Then back up the hill, our eyes now more accustomed to the darkness, noticing the shrubs, bracken and trees growing along the incline. It smelled damp and woody, of rotting leaves and fungi, a smell I loved.

We unbarracked our beds, made them up, put on our striped pyjamas and, carrying our sponge bags, went in groups to the ablutions. We stopped on the way back to read the following day's orders. Whoops of joy—no parades until after dinner. The morning was ours to unpack and familiarize ourselves with the layout of the camp.

We discovered that the majority of the camp buildings, including our billets, were on a plateau. One side sloped to the cookhouse and beyond that to a swimming pool, tennis court and recreational hut for other ranks.

At one edge of the plateau were Married Quarters; behind them another incline led down to the Regimental Offices, gun park and the barrack square. Beyond the square's perimeter stood the garrison cinema, or Gaff. From the cinema there was a narrow sandy path fronting a scanty pine plantation where the Roman Catholic church was. Surrounded as it was by conifers and built of white clapboard with a green trim, it brought to mind a Canadian or New England setting rather than a Southern English one. And not far from the church there was the main road running through the village.

Breda and I blessed ourselves as we passed the church and Katy said, 'Remind me to tell you something about a Catholic church.'

'Tell us now,' I asked.

'I will sometime,' replied Katy as we crossed the road. 'Now I want to have a look at what all this is like.'

What all this was like was a long row of shops. Some with rooms over them, some single-storey and makeshift in appearance. The majority were cafés. More cafés than there were public houses in a Dublin street. Menus were daubed in pipe clay on the windows and chalked on blackboards outside. Sausage and chips. Pie and chips. Whale steak and chips. Pasty and chips. Chips and beans. Cakes, tea, coffee, lemonade and ginger beer.

There was also a post office. A shop selling kitschy souvenirs. Small velvet heart-shaped cushions, satin squares and circles all embroidered in red, royal, emerald, purple and cerise with regimental badges or fond messages to Mum or sweethearts. The messages and shapes were similar to those displayed in the next-door shop, which specialized in tattooing. The tattooist stood in her doorway smoking, a painfully thin woman with garlands of flowers and entwined serpents on her almost fleshless arms. She smiled and said hello. I'd never seen a woman with tattoos before. One of the makeshift shops sold caps and corp badges, sergeants', bombardiers' and lance bombardiers' stripes in sets of three, two and single ones for the lower rank. Amongst these were displayed lanyards, blocks of blanco and bottles of Indian ink with which to whiten stripes. The post office sold newspapers and cigarettes. It was obvious that the shops catered only for military personnel.

We walked up and down the row of shops and cafés looking for variations in the menus, peering in to see which café had jukeboxes, pinball machines. All had, but there was no variety in the menus.

One café was more salubrious in appearance than the others. It was detached and its large window was draped in greyish net curtains. There was no menu visible until closer inspection revealed a hand-written menu tucked inside the curtain resting on the window ledge.

'That's the posh one,' said Katy. 'For the officer cadets. It looks a right dump. No machines, no music. And no other ranks. Not barred, mind you, but discouraged.'

'We won't be missing much,' said Breda. 'Sure the menu's still the same. Chips and chips.'

It was an unwritten law that officer cadets did not fraternize with other ranks, male or female.

Having decided which was our favourite café, we went in for coffee. It was neither better nor worse than what we were accustomed to in the NAFFI. Perry Como was singing on the jukebox, 'Till the End of Time'. It was my first hearing of the song, and I fell in love with it. In future months it was to be my solace when a love affair went wrong. I would sit in the café lingering over a cup of coffee too long so that the owner, a woman, gave me dirty looks, which I brazened out. For if I bought more coffee I could play the record again. And I had to keep hearing Perry's promise of eternal love while willing whoever I was in love with to come through the door; my heart sang along with Perry, 'Till the stars forget to shine I'll go on loving you.' Often he never came through the door. But just as often another tall, handsome soldier did, our eyes met and again for a little time I fell in love.

But all that was still in the future. Today we were exploring, acquainting ourselves with the girls who shared our barrack room. Dry-witted Connie from Manchester was a conscript who couldn't wait for her demobilization, and a Labour supporter who believed that finally the time of the working class had come. Marge from London joked about buying boil plasters to enhance the size of her breasts. In my mind's eye I can still see her when she got out of bed. Standing with her legs crossed, squirming as she tightened her pelvic floor so as not to wet herself. She was the first person I knew who owned a Biro, something none of us had ever seen. A magic pen. Jean was a small plump Scots girl whose face I have never forgotten. She was a clerk in the Admin. Office. She had a pleasant manner but kept to herself. Unlike the rest of us she seldom went to the NAFFI canteen in the evenings and I never knew her to have a date.

* * *

After exploring the village and before our midday meal, I investigated the other descents from the plateau. To reach one of them I passed the gymnasium where in the future I would go to regimental dances and in bad weather have physical training.

Behind the gymnasium was a cricket field and white-painted pavilion. I ran across the pitch and the field beyond it. It seemed to go on forever. And when I reached the edge, I saw a narrow sandy track, its sides lined with peeling-barked silver birch. And at the bottom another scrubby field stretching into the distance. Not worth exploring, I decided, and retraced my steps.

The final descent was close to the billet and very steep, falling down into a place of trees so closely packed their trunks weren't visible. Their tops were bedecked with multi-coloured autumn leaves as if they were a gigantic bouquet packed into an enormous container. The sun shone on them, the breeze stirred them. I had never seen anything like them. They were beautiful, magnificent. I wanted to go down the steep slope, walk amongst them. Feel and hear the leaves crunch beneath my feet. But I guessed it was almost dinner-time. My exploration must wait for another time. But explore it I would.

* * *

Katy worked in the Admin. Office and Breda moved from clerical duties to work with me as a telephonist. Here, as in Catterick Camp, the telephone exchange was part of the guardroom and the guardroom a replica of the one in Yorkshire. Here there were several prison cells along a narrow corridor and several soldiers confined for short spells for less than heinous offences.

They polished and bumpered the floors, renewed the buckets of coke, whitewashed the border boulders, brassoed the cannon and at various times during the days were marched to other parts of the camp on fatigues.

One of my great loves I met while he was a prisoner. A tall, blonde, bronzed Scot who had fought in the Western Desert and Monte Casino.

When he had served his sentence we dated. His name was Steve. He used to sing to me, 'My love is like a red, red rose, that's newly sprung in June.' I can still see him. His lovely fair hair, his blue eyes and his slender broad-shouldered body, his battle-dress bedecked with campaign medals. My rebel soldier who kicked against the discipline of the peacetime army. And I hear him singing, 'And I will come again my love though it were ten thousand miles.'

* * *

The camp, its surroundings, the girls, the village street, the priest, Sunday mass, everything enchanted me. I had never known such happiness. One Sunday after mass a man approached myself and Breda. He was good-looking, oldish, Irish and charming. He invited us to go and meet his wife, who had just moved into married quarters. We went and I tasted Nescafé for the first time. There was a small, beautiful child of three. I fell in love with her, her father, Sean, and gorgeous mother, Betty with the shining cap of golden hair, fat and beautiful, who had been a beautician and hairdresser in a prestigious Newcastle department store. She cut and styled my hair. Suddenly it was beautiful. A nut-brown short page-boy which kept its shape. For the first time ever I was complimented on it. Men in the canteen would touch the shining cap and say, 'You've got smashing hair, Pad.'

* * *

Only Bubbles answered letters properly, replying to what you'd written. She was engaged to her Yank and preparing to become a GI bride. Undergoing medical tests and investigations into her background. She hadn't heard from Deirdre so couldn't give me her new address. Edith and Marj's letters were short. They told of smashing times with blokes and little else, though Edith did give an explanation as to what a technical virgin was. 'It's a prick-teaser. Getting a bloke too worked up and then calling it quits. You could get yourself raped or murdered.' I was as wise as before. Her letters and Marj's were signed across the back of the envelopes T.T.F.N.— Ta, ta for now. Deirdre's would have been embellished with S.A.G.—Saint Anthony guide. Soldiers' love letters were frequently S.W.A.L.K.—sealed with a loving kiss.

* * *

One day I related Deirdre's story to Breda and Katy. Afterwards
Breda coaxed Katy to tell us about the Catholic church she had
mentioned on the first day we arrived in camp.

'Oh, that, it was nothing really.'

'Tell us anyway,' Breda insisted.

'I was living with my granny at the time and she sometimes
ran out of money for the electric.' She laughed. 'Ran out of it
in the pub. So most nights we had to have candles. Little ones
that lasted no time. Anyway I had this mate, Georgie, a
Catholic, and sometimes I'd go into his kirk with him. And one
day I saw these great big candles on the altar. Enormous they
were and I decided to nick one for my granny. Georgie was petrified. They were blessed, he said. He'd go to Hell, to a refor-
matory. I didn't care where he went. All I could think of was
my granny's face when she saw the candle and how I'd be able
to read by it.' She stubbed out her cigarette and lit a new one.
'I made him help me. He was greetin' all the time. We had a
hell of a job lowering it and then getting it out of the holder.'

'Georgie said, "We'll be charged, the polis will arrest us. You
canna carry that through the street." But we did, carried and
dragged it. It was bigger than us. Anyway we got it home.'

'Was your granny delighted?' asked Breda.

'Like hell she was. She skelped me and Georgie. Wouldn't
answer the door in case it was the police.' The beautiful altar
candles. I could picture them. Smell them. See altar boys snuff-
ing them out. See Katy going on to the altar forbidden to
women. Understand Georgie's fears. And at the same time I
laughed at the thought of Katy dragging the blessed candle
through the streets of Edinburgh.

'What did your granny do with it?' I asked. 'Threw it out?'

'Wrapped it in an old quilt, pushed it under the bed and
waited.'

'For what?' I asked.

'Till she was sure the police wouldn't find out who nicked it.
Afterwards she fixed it in an umbrella stand. It was great. I
could read all night and she said it brought us luck.'

'What about Georgie?'

'He didn't play with me again. Poor wee Georgie. He was

one of the unlucky ones who dropped at Arnhem.'

When Katy finished the story she came back again to Deirdre's dilemma, asking me, 'Did you ever ask anyone about Lupinbeds?'

'A few people on the Isle of Man,' I replied shrugging, 'but no luck.'

'You could try the post corporal.'

'Katy, you know I can't stand him.'

'Who can? He's a creep. But think of all the directories, maps and charts he has.'

'He's bound to have heard of it,' Breda said, and reluctantly I agreed to try Charley.

And so the next day I went to see him, thinking as I walked to the post room about Edith's letter and 'prick-teasers'. I was familiar with the word. You got pricks from thorns and pins, and occasionally since I had joined up my conscience had pricked me. I knew Edith wasn't referring to any of those. I had deduced that it was something to do with sex. That mysterious, tantalizing subject. Maybe it was another name for what in Ireland was called a mickey, a flute, a tool, sometimes a pump. If a tool and a mickey were the same thing, then Army Tool-Softener was also to do with sex. But why a softener, I wondered, as I neared Charley's lair.

I was almost there when I remembered the day in work I found what I thought was a banana balloon in a jacket left in for alterations. How the woman working with me had knocked it out of my hand. Kicked it away, ordered me to get a brush and dustpan. Sweep it up and then scrub my hands. If mickeys, flutes and tools were men's things then maybe they covered them with long balloons. But why? Maybe if they had bad kidneys to stop them wetting their trousers. Though this seemed odd, as I remembered seeing baby boys being changed and little boys peeing. Their things were tiny. Like little fat worms. Still I supposed they'd grow as the boys did. But not that much. What I'd found in the judge's pocket was several inches long with plenty of stretch in it. I was almost at Charley's and put the subject out of my mind. I needed a clear head to deal with sneering, jeering Charley.

TEN

Charley was the only male who slept on the plateau. In a room off the one in which he sorted the mail. No one liked him except his girlfriend, Marilyn. Marilyn, it was rumoured, spent more time in the post room than it took to enquire if there were any letters for her. It was also said that she visited it when it was officially closed and had been seen leaving it early in the mornings. She and Charley looked alike. Big, with lumpy features and skin seldom exposed to the light, grey skin reminding one of woodlice turned out from under a stone. They had identical Mona Lisa sneering grins and 'I know something you don't' expressions.

I never went to the post room without Charley making suggestive remarks in what he believed was an Irish accent. Always in his presence I was aware of being what my mother described as, 'a fine, big, soft girl'. But needs must when the devil drives, so in I went to ask about Lupinbeds.

He eyed me up and down and in the Irish accent asked what he could do for me. Not a thing, I thought, looking at his slack mouth and leery eyes. But I smiled and asked if he had ever heard of Lupinbeds.

'Of course I have, Pad, we ain't all Oirish you know.'

I ignored the jibe and asked where it was.

'It,' he said, 'what d'ye mean it?' His mouth was spitty. 'Bedad and begorrah there's millions of them, isn't there one outside the guardroom door.'

'Look,' I said, trying not to show my annoyance. 'I'm serious. I'm trying to find this place.'

'Some bloke I suppose. Hope you didn't do anything you shouldn't. You've been taken for a ride,' he guffawed. 'Lupinbeds, you'll have a bloody hard job finding him at that address.'

'It isn't about a bloke. It's a girl I know. She's trying to find someone.' I was near to tears. Tears of anger and loathing.

'Pull the other one,' he laughed again. I turned to leave.

'Hang on,' he said, 'don't get your knickers in a twist.' I blushed. Men didn't mention knickers.

'You look a bit of alright when you're worked up. Are you serious about this place?'

'Of course I'm serious.'

'Never know with the Oirish. What did you do, see it written down or only hear it?'

'Both. My friend said it. We thought it was a queer sort of name. But then we saw it in a letter. Printed in capital letters. Do you know where it is?'

'Bet you a pound to a penny your mate's looking for Luton.'

'Where's that?'

'Luton's in Beds. See the trouble of having beds on the brain lands you in? Luton's a town in the County of Bedfordshire. Don't suppose you've heard of that either. Tell your mate. Not all that far from here. Expect she's up the pole, eh?'

I thanked him and left. Repeating as I went, 'Lupinbeds. Luton. Beds.' And admitting that the Irish, some anyway, Deirdre, her mother, me and the fella who'd passed on the address, were eejits.

I was still laughing when I got back to the barrack room and told Katy.

'Chinese whispers,' she said, continuing to paint her nails.

'Chinese whispers, what are they?' She blew on her colourless varnish, waved her hands about and got off the bed.

'How messages passed from one place to another become garbled. For instance a message went out on an army radio, "send reinforcements we're going to advance". By the time it was relayed several times it came over as "send three and fourpence we're going to a dance".'

'As true as God?'

'That's how the story goes.'

I thought it was hilarious and went into another kink of laughing. Then became serious wondering how I could get the news to Deirdre. Breda had come in in the meantime. She suggested sending it to her home in Dublin. 'I never knew where she lived,' I said.

'Well then send it to her last army one. So long as you've got her army number right she'll get it.'

I did that; whether she received it or not I never knew, never heard from her again. Occasionally when I was home on leave I'd wonder, as I walked up Grafton Street or down O'Connell Street, whether I'd bump into Deirdre. I never did. But many years later when once again I was a civilian I learned the outcome of the marriage that had only lasted six weeks.

* * *

One Sunday towards the end of November, Katy, Breda and I were in the recreation room listening to 'Two-Way Family Favourites'.

The room was comfortably furnished with an assortment of easy chairs, piles of magazines, a wireless and table-tennis equipment. On this particular day only the three of us were present. Katy was smoking. Breda was knitting her father's Christmas present, a pair of navy socks, from a jumper she had unravelled. I was attempting to make a pair of French knickers from parachute silk. As far as I knew, every girl in the camp owned a length of parachute silk and was attempting to make pieces of lingerie. Where the creamy white silk material came from I don't remember. Perhaps there were girls courting paratroopers. Perhaps there was a spiv flogging it, though I can't recall ever handing over money. That would have been almost impossible, as my pay was invariably spent almost immediately after pay parade on my sweet ration, fifty duty-free cigarettes, soap, toothpaste and whichever cleaning agent for buttons or shoes I was about to run out of.

Breda knitted furiously and talked incessantly. About everything and anything. What she'd said to Father Tom after Mass, what he'd said to her. How the socks were progressing. Would she remember how to turn the heels. Relating her previous disastrous attempts at knitting.

Frank Sinatra, Perry Como, Anne Shelton, Vera Lyn and Bing Crosby sang our favourite songs. Joe Loss and Glen Miller played our favourite music and all the time Breda kept up her running commentary. Katy was annoyed. Drumming her fingers on the arm of her chair. And I wanted to listen to the wireless while my mind considered whether I should apply for leave over

Christmas or go home for New Year. Every time I had almost reached a decision Breda demanded my attention. 'You've got to listen to this,' she'd say, or ask for help picking up one of the many stitches she dropped.

Reaching a decision as to which period of leave I would apply for was complicated. Breda and I couldn't both be away from the telephone exchange at the same time, except for a period of one day when the Regimental Police in the guardroom would man the board. Though knowing Breda's generosity I felt sure that if I spun a yarn of my mother banking on me being home for Christmas she would settle for leave at New Year.

Parting from Steve was the real stumbling-block. Being Scottish he would be going to Glasgow for Hogmanay. That meant if I spent the festive season in Dublin we'd be separated for twenty days.

How could I exist so long without him? I'd probably die of a broken heart. My beautiful, wonderful man. How could I live without his kisses, his embraces, the compliments he paid me? How would I supplement the suppers he bought me, the cups of 'char and wads' in the canteen, my admission into the cinema in the days after I returned from leave and he was still in Scotland? In those long-ago days men paid for everything and always offered you their cigarettes.

Breda's voice was like a chain-saw. I began again to think about Steve. At the same moment Bing began to croon, 'I'm Dreaming of a White Christmas', a favourite of mine. Breda began reminiscing about how and when she had seen the picture for the first time. Giggling about the fella who had taken her. Kept her out late and the row she had had with her mother. 'It was a scream, honest to God.'

Katy looked as if she was about to scream, her fingers making staccato sounds on the chair's arm. My chain of memories was wrecked. I could listen to a song and think at the same time, but not when Breda was competing. And yet because I was so fond of her I couldn't say, 'Shut up, knock it off, give it a rest.' Sometimes Katy did. But today she used a more subtle method of gaining a respite. 'Do us a favour, Breda. Nip over to the village and buy a *News of the World*.'

'That's a great idea. I was getting a bit restless,' replied Breda, stabbing the ball of navy wool with her steel needles. 'I might meet someone for a chat.'

When she was gone Katy and I looked at each other and laughed. She picked up another magazine and I recalled meeting Steve for the first time.

* * *

My beloved rebel. He came to polish the exchange floor as part of his fatigues. He carried a piece of blanket and a two-pound tin that had once held plums filled with polish. A stick stuck up out of it. With his other hand he dragged a bumper. He acknowledged me with a nod and began on the floor, flicking lumps of polish onto it with the stick. Wielding the bumper to spread it, then placing the piece of blanket beneath it and bringing a shine to the floor. Between answering calls I watched him. His back was to me and I admired his neat little bum. Now and then he straightened up to rest and smoke. We talked. I asked him why he was in detention.

'For dumb insolence.'

'What's dumb insolence?'

'A look in your eye.'

'You're pulling my leg.'

'Straight up. It's looking unafraid into the eyes of a superior rank.'

'Really?'

'Really. Interpreted by officers and NCOs as disrespect and defiance.'

'And was it in your case?'

'Too bloody right it was. A stupid, ignorant sergeant didn't like the layout of my kit for inspection and asked what I had to say for myself. If I told him I'd have finished up in the glasshouse. So I just looked at him.'

He had the most beautiful pale blue eyes which were smiling at me as he spoke. But I could imagine them turned on someone he disliked. See them change to cold hard slivers of ice. Piercing, threatening eyes.

'How long did you get?'

'Three days. It was worth it.'

'You sound as if you don't like the army.'

'I don't. Not in peacetime. Petty-minded morons. The army's the most class-ridden institution left.'

When he had brought the floor up to the required shine he

asked me if I'd go out with him. Having instantly fallen in love, I agreed.

* * *

On our first date I met him after tea. We went for a walk. We talked about ourselves. He was going to university after demob to read medicine. It was a cold clear starry night. He told me to look at the sky and pointed out constellations and named them. Until that moment, apart from the evening star I hadn't known stars had names.

Holding hands we walked to the village café, ate the greasy chips, drank liquids that could have been tea, coffee or artificially sweetened washing-up water, smoked, played the pinball machine and jukebox and gazed into each other's eyes. Then left to find a dark sheltered place, where to protect me from the cold Steve undid his greatcoat, took it off and laid it round my shoulders. We kissed such kisses. My head reeled, a tingle ran down to my toes. He stroked my face and said my skin felt like a peach. He was so tall I barely reached his chest. So tall and so strong, making me feel fragile and cherished.

* * *

Breda came back with the newspaper. 'You have a read of it first,' she said handing it to Katy. The radio programme was drawing to a close, playing out with a Jimmy Shand melody. All our feet tapped in time to the lively music. 'Roll on Hogmanay,' said Katy, switching off the wireless and beginning to read the paper.

'The bastard!' she then exclaimed vehemently and laid down the paper. 'He should be strung up.'

'Who? What did he do?' Breda wanted to know.

'Raped a wee lassie. Fifteen she was.'

'I've always been meaning to ask someone about rape. Like what it is exactly?'

'You don't know?' said Katy, laying down the paper and reaching for her packet of Four Castles.

'I do sort of,' Breda blushed and giggled and I was all ears, not knowing either what rape was. 'I have an idea only I'm not sure if I've got it right.' I could tell by her face she was regretting raising the subject. I kept quiet.

93

'Tell us what you know, Breda.' Breda looked away from Katy, who winked at me. She was as fond of Breda as I was but could never resist egging her on to reveal her naïveté. Breda fell for it every time.

'Well,' she said, 'it's when, you know, when a fella gets fresh. Puts his tongue in your mouth. Ah, Katy, you're having me on. You know what I mean.'

'Sticking his tongue in your mouth is often how it starts. Though it could begin with a punch in the jaw, a kick or a blow that would knock you down, kill you.'

'Katy, d'ye think I'm an eejit or something?' Breda laughed nervously. 'There's no green in my eye.'

I felt sorry for Breda but my curiosity was avid. Katy was about to describe rape.

'A man has a prick. What he pees from. A soft, limp worm-like thing until he gets worked up. Then it begins to grow. Longer and harder. And some bastards will do anything to get it inside a woman.'

'Oh my God,' Breda whispered. She looked as if she was about to faint. 'Oh, Sacred Heart of Jesus. I told my mother that.'

'Told your mother what?'

'About rape, about girls being raped. Only I never knew what it was.' She started snivelling. In a minute she'd be really crying. Before she started I got in a question.

'What happens after he goes inside a woman?'

'I didn't think you were thick as well,' said Katy. 'He pumps away at you and after a while he comes.'

'Comes?'

'Yeah, shoots his load, white, sticky stuff. It makes you pregnant.'

I persisted, ignoring Breda's audible sobs. 'Is that only with rape?'

'No, it happens with a normal bloke, one not usually out to kill you.'

Breda was sobbing loudly. Katy and I went to her, offering hankies, soothing words, Katy's soon becoming terse as she said, 'Stop greetin' and tell us what's the matter. Control yourself for God's sake. Anyone passing will think we're knocking you about, tell us what it is.' In between kinks of laughter verging on the hysterical, Breda told us.

'She wants me to desert. Every time I go home that's all I

hear. "Get out of them forces. You're not going back. From Ireland you don't have to … I'll lock you up if you don't."'

'But why does your mother keep saying that?' I asked.

'Because I told her about the rapes.'

'What rapes?' Katy shook her. 'What rapes, Breda? Blow your nose. Have a fag.'

'But I don't smoke …' Breda protested.

'One drag'll calm you down.' Katy pushed a cigarette between Breda's lips. She gagged, coughed then took a deep breath and told us a story.

'It happened when I was in basic training. Canadians invited us to a dance in their mess. It was smashing. Gorgeous food. Square dancing, you know, that's like Irish dancing. We were having a great time. And then the lights went out. A power cut. We often had power cuts. Then there were screams. Girls screaming. The lights came on again. A few girls were crying. I didn't know them. Like they weren't in our squad. But anyway our sergeant got us all together and we had to leave. In the truck going back to camp everyone was talking. Saying what had happened. And some said that girls had been raped. The next time I wrote home I told my mother about it.'

'You told your mother girls had been raped?' asked Katy, 'Why, for God's sake?'

'For something to say. I'm no good at writing letters.'

'No wonder she's demented. No wonder she wants you out of the forces. Did anything ever come out of the girls who were supposed to be raped?'

'I never heard any more about it.'

'They probably had their bums pinched. You've got to write home and put your mother straight.'

Breda looked at Katy. A horrified expression on her face.

'I couldn't mention such a thing to my mother now that I know what it means.'

'Suit yourself,' said Katy. 'I want some fresh air. Let's go to the village.'

On the way I was busy putting two and two together. Now I knew what a prick was. What an Army Tool-Softener was and why my mother had threatened to kill me when she saw the white stains on my dark brown coat. And I thought what a frightening and at the same time exciting thing sex was.

ELEVEN

Breda came to relieve me, her face beaming. 'Wait'll you hear the news, kid. My Da's ship is docking on December 28th. I haven't seen him for ages. I'd love to be home then. But only if it's OK with you.'

'Why wouldn't it be?'

'Steve will still be in camp?'

'Only until the next day.'

'I know but if you go home for Christmas you'll be separated for a good while. I won't mind if you want your leave for New Year, honest to God.'

Sometimes I wondered if anyone could be always as obliging as Breda. Always willing to accommodate others. Did she fume inwardly? Feel put upon? Wish she could be more assertive?

She never gave offence. Shared whatever she had. Swapped shifts to suit me. Never complained if I was late relieving her.

Watching her get ready to take over the switchboard, seeing her open smiling face, any doubts were swept away. She was genuinely incapable of resentment, bitterness, envy. It was no wonder everyone liked her. 'Listen,' I said, taking off the headphones from round my neck. 'You go and see your dad. Three weeks won't kill me without Steve. My mother might if I don't go home for Christmas.'

'Are you certain?'

'Definitely.' And so it was agreed. And once my application for leave, signed 'your obedient servant', was in and granted, my thoughts turned to Christmases in Dublin.

I remembered all the good things about them. The buzz there was. You could feel it in the air. See it wherever you looked. In the shops. Little ones, their windows decorated with daubs of cotton wool, hung with gaudy paper chains. Glitzy ones in Grafton Street into which you could look but never step over the threshold. Everything sold there was beyond the reach of the working class. But the beautiful gowns, luxurious furs, lingerie in pure silk and satin could be admired, marvelled at, imagined against your skin as you gazed through the plate-glass windows.

Moore Street, Henry Street and Thomas Street jumping with life. The dealers calling encouragement to buy. Bargains galore. Paper chains, balloons and baubles. Pyramids of apples and oranges.

Macey's, Cassidy's and Kellet's in George's Street, Aladdin's caves of artificial silk and stockinette slips and knickers. Angora boleros. Coats and hats, frocks and skirts. Up-to-the-minute in fashion at prices that were affordable for factory and office girls who'd paid into money clubs.

And all the knick-knacks. Powder compacts, manicure sets, workboxes, brush and comb sets in imitation tortoiseshell. In imitation leather cases. Gifts for aunties, nieces and friends.

The chemist's windows filled with bottles of scent. Evening in Paris in its blue flask and pictures of the Eiffel Tower. Phul Nana—hints of the mysterious East about its wrapping—and riotously coloured bottles of Californian Poppies.

Outside butcher's shops geese and turkeys hung suspended by their feet, fully feathered round their necks, the snowy down blood-stained. The glazed eyes gazing unseeingly. The smell of their flesh, of their undrawn innards. There were smoked and unsmoked hams, halves and whole, ox tongues lolling on enamel trays, silverside, brisket and tail-end of corned beef steeping in barrels of brine. And on the south side of the city, from Aungier Street, wafting through the narrow streets and alleys as far as Saint Stephen's Green, the rich smell of Jacob's Oxford Lunches baking. And at home my mother would be checking the ingredients for her Christmas pudding. Ingredients bought over many weeks in small quantities and hidden about the house to stop them being raided by my brother and sister and me when our sweet tooth got the better of us.

The flurry of activity as she washed the currants and raisins, chopped the candied peel, grated nutmegs, measured out spice. Mixing and stirring the lump of suet to be shredded, the pudding cloth to be boiled and greased. The mixing and stirring.

Her regrets that she wouldn't have time to slap up a few rolls of wallpaper. Her frenzied air, her frantic movements. The beast on her back that drives women in the run-up to Christmas into believing that unless presents were wrapped, food prepared, the house cleaned, and the holly and the ivy behind the pictures, Christmas Day wouldn't arrive.

My mother shedding tears as she recalled our Christmas trees from Mount Jerome. Depressed one minute, manic the next. Laughing and singing. Fortifying herself with another cup of strong, sweet tea. Wind surging in her stomach from not stopping for a meal.

Racking her brains as to how she could afford a present for us. Recalling the last Christmas before my father died. Her eyes filling with tears, her voice hoarse with sadness as she said, 'Nearly three years buried and no still no stone over him.' Her spirits lifting and an expectant look on her face as she heard the rattle of the letter box and hurried into the hall to see what the postman had delivered. Never opening the letters until she had studied the handwriting, postmarks and stamps. Second guessing who they were from as she turned them over several times. An English or American stamp would transform her face with an expression of joyful expectancy.

She'd take out the cards and letters and put them aside as she peered into the envelopes for cheques or dollars. Finding none she'd search the cards and letters. If there was no money she'd say of my English grandfather, 'The mean old bastard, wouldn't you think he'd remember his orphaned grandchildren. And he wallowing in it. Money that your father helped him make.'

The oversight of the American relations was forgiven, for often during the year they did send dollars. And she'd console herself. 'The money could be delayed in the post because of the war. Maybe it'll arrive after Christmas.' Her disappointment was for us. For what we'd be deprived of. The fancy socks from Cassidy's in O'Connell Street for me, a doll for my sister and a tool set or bus driver's uniform for my brother. For herself she wanted nothing. Only to have the means to surprise and delight us on Christmas morning.

But she lived in hope. Speculating aloud as to what the grocer would give her for a present. 'Maybe this year it'll be an iced cake, though they're like sawdust. Can't hold candlelight to one from the Monument Creamery. And if not a cake surely to God a thick fat red candle. If he insults me again with a calendar that you can buy anywhere for tuppence I'll tell him what to do with it. And I'll never spend another farthing in his shop.'

We never had poultry for Christmas. Only once in a relation's home had I tasted turkey. Our dinner was half a Roscrea ham given by an aunt. After boiling and skinning it my mother pressed fresh breadcrumbs into its coat of fat and toasted it on a trivet before the fire. With it we sometimes had stuffed steak, a thick piece of round which she slashed to make a pocket and filled with delicious stuffing before stitching up the cut. Jelly and custard for our pudding. Christmas pudding was served cold, sliced and eaten like cake. And, whether or not the grocer had given her the pink iced confection, there was the cake from the Monument Creamery. Made, as she was fond of telling us, from the best ingredients in the land. And always she managed a present for each of us, no matter how small.

But first and foremost Christmas was a Holy Time celebrating the birth of Christ. Animosities temporarily forgiven if not completely forgotten. Confession and Communion. And for the majority of mothers an early Mass. Before I grew up, which was considered to be when you went to work, I always went with my mother to six o'clock Mass. There must have been mornings when it was misty, when it rained. But in my memories I feel an exhilarating cold. See a sky full of stars as she and I walked to Saint Kevin's in Harrington Street.

The majority of the congregation were women. The majority like my mother had probably been up all night putting the finishing touches to jellies and stuffings, wrapping last-minute gifts, preparing the vegetables for the following day.

The crib was up and the baby Jesus lying in it. All over the country fat red candles would have burned on window sills from which the curtains were drawn back to light His way.

There was another memory of Christmas; smiling to myself I recalled it. I was sixteen and for the first and last time for many years I got drunk. Langers. Legless. Stocious drunk. It was a Christmas Eve and I had been to confession. Before going my mother had told me of the words she had had with her next-door neighbour. 'The cheek of her telling me where and when my son can kick a football. But I was well able for her. Don't you think because my husband's dead you can browbeat me. I'm paying my rent and my child'll kick his ball wherever he likes. An oul' bull driver, that's what she is. And don't you ever

99

recognize her again. D'ye hear me?' she called after me as I went out of the room.

Passing the neighbour's house on the way back from confession she tapped the window and beckoned to me. I went to her hall door and knocked. 'It's open,' she called, 'come in, love.' She and my mother rowed constantly and each time I was forbidden to recognize her ever again. They seldom stayed bad friends for long and in any case I would have ignored the ban. I was very fond of the woman. She was warm-hearted and could always make me laugh. Barely five foot with a face as wrinkled as a tortoise. Never without a cigarette in her mouth and the smell of drink about her. She had done a stretch in prison for robbing money from a house where she cleaned. She told me about it.

'Ten shillings, that's all it was. For a horse. A dead cert. I put three on the horse and released Jack's suit from the pawn. He had to have it for a cousin's wedding the next day. If the horse had come in I'd have put the fecking ten-shilling note back. Imagine the badness of some people. Reporting it to the police. Anyway I got on great with the wardress. She never saw me short of a smoke. "You've an honest face," she said, "I know I can trust you. Not like some of them in here. A gang of robbers the lot of them."'

She brought me into the parlour, a small over-furnished room with a blazing turf fire and festooned with garish paper chains in honour of the season. 'Did your mammy say anything about the words we had?' she asked while pouring red liquid from a bottle.

She filled two tumblers. It wasn't Vimto nor red lemonade. There weren't any bubbles. 'She said something about a football,' I said, taking the proffered glass.

'She's very hasty. Sure I meant nothing by it. My fella's an oul' divil about footballs. Anyone would think he was never a child himself. So tell her I'm sorry. That's why I called you in so you could give her my message. Drink that, it'll do you good. A drop of port wine's good for young girls.' She sat down beside me. I liked the taste of the wine. It was very sweet.

'How are ye getting on in work?'

I told her. She'd worked at the tailoring and knew some of the older women in my factory. I kept sipping the drink while we talked. And she kept topping me up. I felt in great humour. Laughing at everything she said. Then I began to feel sleepy.

'It's the heat of the fire. Take off your coat, you must be roasting,' she advised.

'I won't, thanks all the same. I'd better go in. I've been gone this long time.'

'I've got a little present for you. I'll slip in in the morning and bring your mammy a taste of my pudding and the presents. I've got something for the children as well,' she said at the door. 'Goodnight and God bless you.'

My head felt queer. A lightness in it. And the few yards to my own house had me walking crookedly. I reached through the letter-box, pulled up the string with the key attached. The key didn't slip in easily. I was fumbling with it. Then I knocked with the knocker. My mother opened the door. There was no light in the hall. She couldn't see me properly until I was in the kitchen. When she did she shouted, 'Where were you? Who have you been with?' I started to giggle. 'I'll tell you tomorrow,' I laughed loudly and swayed. 'I'm going to bed now.' I began to strip off. For a few seconds she stared in amazement at what I was doing. Undressing was something you only did in privacy and with great modesty.

'Sacred Heart of Jesus!' she exclaimed. 'You've been drinking intoxicating liquor. Look at you standing there in your skin. Thanks be to God your brother isn't here.'

I was stripped down to my woollen vest, yellowed from many washings and shrunken so that inches of my bum were exposed. Her hand slapped it hard. 'Get into the bedroom.' She followed me, her hand slapping, slapping my bare skin. Her voice, which sounded far away, telling me I'd never be able to hold my head up again. I was destroyed. I was a drunkard. And I kept on laughing and she slapping. 'Wait'll the morning,' she threatened. 'Wait'll it's daylight. I'll kill you, so I will.'

I collapsed on the bed. The ceiling came down to meet me and I thought I was going to die. My stomach heaved. I lifted the corner of the mattress and vomited through the bed springs. Then I fell asleep. She woke me roughly. My head was on fire, bursting with pain. 'Get up this minute. The smell is turning my stomach.'

In my shrunken vest exposing a nakedness I was now embarrassedly aware of, I got up and began looking for my clothes.

'Put that on you,' she said, handing me a dressing-gown, 'and go in to the kitchen.'

Sitting by the fire I could smell Jeyes Fluid as she washed away the vomit.

She had calmed down and when eventually she brought me hot, sweet tea her interrogation began. Her bluey-grey eyes bored into me, making it almost impossible to lie. And in the long run I told her where I'd had a drink.

'The curse of God on her trying to corrupt my daughter. But wait till morning.' Then she launched into the perils of drink. All the men and women destroyed by it. The broken homes. Neglected children. 'And remember this, a drunken woman is a sorrier sight than a man face-falling. For a drunken woman neglects her home and worse still her children. The curse of God on that oul' reprobate to try and lead you astray. Will you be well enough to come to six o'clock mass? After your carousing you won't be able to receive. But God will forgive you.'

It would be at least ten years before the ceiling ever came down to meet me again.

TWELVE

ATSs travelling alone at night by boat went first class. First class on the Irish Mail boats, fifty years ago, was travelling in style. And style I admired, even at a distance. I had sampled it the previous night. Spending seven shillings and sixpence for a berth on the Euston-to-Holyhead train; for a further one and sixpence booking tea when we arrived at the port; grandiosely tipping the steward one shilling. That already an eighth of my two weeks' pay and ration money was squandered caused me not the slightest worry.

On board the ship I settled myself in a lounge of chintzy sofas, deep armchairs, occasional tables and hovering stewards awaiting a beck and call.

The dining-room was furnished to the same standard. Breakfast was delicious. The fact that soon after docking an identical breakfast would be put before me caused me no concern. Money, when you had it, was for spending.

On the train into Westland Row each familiar landmark made my heart leap with joy and once past Ringsend Basin I was up leaning out of the window looking for sight of my mother.

And there she was on the platform as smart and elegant as ever. Wearing high heels, a slim-fitting coat and a little hat tilted over one eye. She had a head and face that could carry hats. Any hat. I'd watch her push it this way and that. Bend or tilt up the brim, set it on one side of her head or the other, all the while studying her image in the glass until it was to her liking.

At first sight of her my heart filled with love. Then she was holding me, kissing me, letting me go and, for the attention of anyone within earshot likely to be interested or impressed, asking me, 'Have you been foreign?' I could have killed her. 'Shut up,' I hissed. 'You're making a show of me.' She smiled, displaying the gold teeth amongst her false ones as if I'd paid her a compliment. Full of affectation as always. Crucifying me with embarrassment. Plying me with more questions about my foreign travels. Hoping for an audience. Then a man bumped into her and she rounded on him. 'You should look where you're going. You could have knocked me under the train.' 'Bloody blind oul' booby,' she said when he was out of earshot. We both laughed. That was my mother. My erratic, volatile, warm-hearted, generous mother.

'You must be jaded,' she said, picking up my case. 'We'll get a cab.'

She had a chat with the jarvey before we got into the cab. Telling me, as we leant against the musty-smelling leather seats, that years ago she used to dance with him. That he had been mad about her. According to her, every man had been mad about her years ago.

As we drove up Westland Row she took out her powder compact and studied her face, something she always did after friendly contact with a man. Any man, the gas or electricity men come to empty the meters, the postman or one delivering coal. 'You must be in the money,' I said as she put away the compact. 'We could have got the bus.'

'I am. Wait'll I tell you. Bernard advised me to settle out of court. I was awarded £25.' Bernard was a childhood friend, now her solicitor.

'What action was that?' I asked. There had been so many I'd lost count.

'For the food poisoning I got. Remember the quarter of cooked ham. I'd diarrhoea and vomiting for three days. Nearly killed. I wouldn't mind only I gave the oul' bester a chance. Dying on my feet I went to the shop to complain. Wouldn't refund my money. I soon showed him what your mother is made of. Dying and all as I was, down to the City Analyst I went with the ham. Every tin in the shop was condemned. We'll have a grand Christmas on the head of it. Wait'll you see your presents.'

Shopkeepers who sold inferior food or the Corporation who didn't maintain the paths causing her to fall off her high heels—she sued them all. The Irish were ever a litigious race.

My brother and sister had minded the fire. It blazed merrily and the big iron kettle sang on the hob. They had grown, changed in the time I'd been away. My sister nearly twelve, beginning to titivate herself. My brother sixteen, out of Synge Street School, where, despite the charitable Brothers having taken him without fees, the cost of second-hand textbooks defeated even my mother's resourcefulness. He had the promise of a job in a small upholstery factory.

They kissed and hugged me. Said Christmas without me wouldn't have been the same.

After showing what she had bought for me—an enamelled compact and a pair of kid gloves—my mother began to cook breakfast, regaling me with tales of the neighbours while she punctured Hafner's sausages, snipped bacon rinds and basted eggs. Starting a story about the woman next door, who'd been in prison again. Halfway through relating the incident she remembered another happening which took precedence over the prison saga and launched into it.

'But what happened to Mrs James?' I asked.

'Oh, wait'll you hear the outcome of that,' she replied, dishing up the food. And began a third story so that as we sat to eat three stories were on the go. Without a doubt I knew I was home.

What with the journey and two breakfasts inside me I wanted to sleep. Before lying down I was relaxing with a cigarette when she launched an attack about the dependant's allowance, accusing me of not having applied for it. Which I countered with the fact she'd had a letter stating she didn't qualify.

'You could have got someone to write that. Some co-whiffler in the office.'

'That's not true.'

'Then tell me how everyone I know with a son or daughter gets an allowance.'

'How do I know?' I said and stifled a yawn. The surfeit of food and her voice, which hadn't stopped talking since we met, were making me long for the oblivion of sleep.

'Know well you do,' she retorted.

'I'm going to lie down.'

'Don't, not for a minute. Not until I put a hot jar in the bed.'

* * *

I went to see the girls in the factory. In the narrow filthy cloak-room we talked and talked. They came down from the workroom a few at a time so as not to arouse the manager's suspicion. They listened and questioned. Gasped then laughed about Poles who bit off nipples. I described the horrible food and the uniform you wouldn't want to be found dead in. In turn they told me about their lives and loves. About boys and girls I had known who were in sanatoriums dying. About those who had died. I described the beautiful camp, the abundance of gorgeous men, the swimming-pool and tennis court. I showed them a photograph of Steve. They admired him. And all the while I was thinking how lucky I was to have escaped. Wondering how I could have been relatively contented working in the factory.

The girls went back to work. I promised to come and see them again. Jennie lingered after the others had left. She was a loner. Not from choice. A bit of a dope, was how she was described. What Edith and Marj would have called gormless. I'd had very little to do with her and was surprised when she asked if I'd go to the pictures with her on Saturday afternoon. I couldn't think of an excuse and agreed. We arranged a time to meet.

The film was *On the Road to Morocco* starring Bing Crosby, Dorothy Lamour and Bob Hope. The cinema was the Savoy. The ceiling replicated a portion of a starry sky. The cloakroom was warm, scented, furnished with full-skirted dressing tables. There was fragrant liquid soap, mirror tiles and deep carpets. If you never saw the film, the cloakroom made the price of admission worthwhile.

Jennie insisted on paying for the tickets. Knowing how little she earned I was surprised, but relieved at the same time, for I had not much money.

Before the picture started a magnificent brightly-lit Wurlitzer organ slowly emerged from somewhere beneath the orchestra pit and played a selection of popular songs. The audience sang along aided by the words flashed on the screen. The atmosphere was magical. The stars above, the music, the luxury. The air redolent of women's scent and face powder, of chocolate, sweets and oranges. A sense of joyful anticipation. Bing crooned, 'Moonlight becomes you, it goes with your hair'. Dorothy's cloud of glorious hair flowed round her sinuous body in its captivating sarong. And I promised myself that when I finished in the ATS I'd grow my hair like Dorothy's. I wanted to watch the picture a second time round. I whispered this to Jennie, who whispered back, 'You can't, I'm taking you for tea.'

'Where?' I asked.

'Here, upstairs in the restaurant.'

Tea at the Savoy! That I couldn't turn down. Apart from the dining salon on the boat I had only ever eaten in the village cafés, the NAFFI canteen and Woolworth's in Dublin, chosen by my mother because the delft was sterilized. While you ate you could see the sterilizer in action.

Once when going to balcony seats I had glimpsed the Savoy restaurant. Individual tables, pink shaded lamps and black-suited waiters. I was thrilled at the prospect. Following her up the stairs I asked how she could afford such generosity.

'My uncle's home from England. He gave me two pounds. Only don't let on, you know, not to anyone in work.' I gave her my promise.

I looked through the menu and chose scrambled eggs—the cheapest item I could spot. Followed by delicious cream cakes. Halfway through the meal, she said how much she liked me, how she had always wanted to be my friend. And would I meet her again before I went back. Sorry and grateful though I felt towards her, the lies tripped off my tongue. 'I'd love to, but I've all these relations to see. But I'll write when I get back to England.' I never did.

* * *

Christmas came and went. Relations brought me presents. Bottles of scent, slips and knickers, new rosary beads. And gave me advice. I was to mind myself. Not neglect my duties and write home regularly. And the advice of an old Jewish woman, a neighbour, was to never let a man touch me below the neck.

On Saint Stephen's Day I went to a dance and saw the fella I had believed I had left home for. And wondered what I had ever seen in him. Compared to Steve he was a weedy bit of a thing. Wearing cheap clothes and his hair plastered with Brylcreem. Edith had been right, it wasn't for unrequited love I had left home.

* * *

Now I was ready to leave again. I visited the factory for the second time. But for me and the girls the novelty of my return from England had worn off. Now we had separate lives.

My mother noticed my long face and kept asking what ailed me. Then she hit upon it. 'You can't wait to get back to that den of iniquity. Though how you showed your face here I don't know.'

'What have I done now?' I asked, falling into the trap.

'Ran away and left me penniless. I'm a laughing-stock in the post office. The woman with the big allowance.'

I tried changing the subject by telling her Deirdre's story. She sniffed contemptuously. 'He ran off with someone else,' she said.

'He could have had an accident and lost his memory.'

She laughed derisively. 'He could in his arse.'

I accused her of not being very romantic. 'I was,' she replied. 'When I was your age I was. But the world does things to you.'

Trying to introduce a touch of levity into the conversation I said, 'Maybe you'll be lucky. Maybe you'll fall again or get poisoned and win an action.'

She wasn't amused.

* * *

The first letter my mother wrote after I got back to camp told me that Jennie had been sacked for robbing the petty cash. I was glad I hadn't mentioned the treat. An in-depth interrogation would have followed. Had Jennie confided where she got the money? Why didn't I ask? Where did I think a young wan on small money got the price of the tickets and the tea?

Whenever I brought something into the house, bars of chocolate, lucky bags, every acquisition that she hadn't paid for had to be accounted for in her determination to instil honesty into her children. Followed by grim tales of reformatories, dark cells and diets of bread and water.

* * *

This one and that slipped me shillings and half-crowns, and one very generous relation produced a ten-shilling note. 'For the journey, it'll get you a cup of tea.' The money burned holes in my pockets. Cups of tea was all I could afford. No breakfast in the ship's dining-room. No sleeping car to Euston. I sat up for the six-hour journey. Ate boiled bacon sandwiches, drank cold coffee my mother had put into a bottle and corked with a wad of paper. Travelled across London on the tube blinded and choked by the smoke of dozens of cigarettes. From Waterloo I went to Brookwood where an army truck picked me up and took me and others who had travelled on the same train back to camp.

Katy, Breda and Steve were still on leave. I marked on the calendar their return date, felt guilty I hadn't bought a gift for Steve and the girls. From the girl with the weak bladder I borrowed a few shillings until pay day.

In the afternoon I reported to the guardroom for my telephone duties. Ginger, the regimental police sergeant, was delighted to see me. 'Kid,' he said, 'I never want to answer another bloody phone.'

'I didn't think someone of your rank would have had to. What happened?'

'Half the buggers went sick. Delhi belly. Though if you ask me it was swilling beer over Christmas.'

Ginger was an old soldier, an 'India Man'. Bald, pugnacious-looking. I was afraid of my life of him when we first met. He looked so fierce and had a roar like a jackass. It was, I soon discovered, all bluster. Now I was very fond of him. He didn't approve of me going out with Steve. 'Hope you're not thinking of getting serious,' he said when he found out we were courting. 'That bloke's a bad 'un. Too hot-headed. Lucky if he doesn't finish up in the glasshouse before his demob. You watch it.'

A lot of senior NCOs and Warrant Officers had manners and loud voices similar to Ginger's. They strutted about, deafened you when they gave drill commands to the men. The Regimental Sergeant-Major was such a one. A caricature of a typical regimental sergeant-major. Pot-bellied, straight-backed, as Katy said, 'You'd think he was wearing a surgical spinal support or had a ramrod up his arse.' He had the moustache and high colouring to match the rest of his appearance.

One morning not long after I came to the camp I slept late. Without having breakfast I ran all the way to the guardroom. There he was standing in the exchange, puffed up like a rooster with his cane tucked underneath his arm.

I began to explain. To make excuses. He silenced me. Told me to stand to attention then bawled me out, reducing me to tears. 'The telephone is a vital link in the communications system. It is your duty to man it at 09.00 hours. Nine o'clock,' he thundered. 'Do you understand?' I nodded my head. 'Nine o'clock means nine o'clock sharp, not twenty past. You are guilty of being absent from your post. That is an offence for which you could be placed on a charge.'

I had stopped listening. Fear prevented me from comprehending what he was saying until, lowering his voice slightly, I heard him say, 'And I suppose you missed your breakfast? Well then, speak up.'

'Yes, sir.' And I thought, missing breakfast is probably another chargeable offence like allowing yourself to get severely sunburned. I'd be charged all right.

'Don't ever let it happen again. No second chances,' he said, about-turned and marched out.

Once he had left the guardroom the RPs and Ginger came to comfort me. 'His bark is worse than his bite,' Ginger consoled me. And a lance-corporal said, 'Cheer up, Pad, Taffy'll be back soon with the tea.' Sergeant-major's tea, the best in the army. How I needed a cup of that strong sweet brew.

During the tirade no calls had come through. Now every eyelid in the board was blinking. I felt as if I had two left hands, both stricken with a form of paralysis. I was just beginning to calm down when I glanced out the window. The RSM was marching up the path. He had changed his mind. He was going to charge me. I heard the soldiers in the next room come to attention and saw the door open. I longed for my mother's presence. In the tyrant marched and held out a paper bag. 'The missus sent it,' he said, and marched out again. Inside the bag was a generous triangle of golden-brown Cornish pasty, home-made.

'Told you, didn't I, Pad, his bark's worse than his bite.' Ginger handed me a thick enamel mug brimming with tea.

* * *

Katy, Breda and my beloved had a glorious New Year. Katy and Steve first-footing and partying through the night, Breda in the bosom of her large family, which included an aunt visiting from Boston.

They bought me presents. Katy gave me a miniature book of Robbie Burns's poetry in red tartan. Steve gave me the first piece of jewellery I had ever owned. A silver horseshoe and chain. The horseshoe was encrusted with tiny pearls to look like white heather. But the present which caused me the most excitement was the pair of nylons given by Breda.

I'd never seen nylon stockings before. They were to my eyes like gossamer. Precious beyond words. 'My auntie told me you should keep them in a jam-jar when not wearing them,' Breda informed me and Katy, for whom she had also bought stockings. 'They ladder and snag easy. In a drawer they could get caught up in something else.'

I listened to their tales of revelry slightly enviously. In camp the night had passed with little celebration. Even so it was better than being in Dublin. For ours wasn't a house that celebrated New Year. We would stand by the front door listening to the bells of Christchurch Cathedral ring the old year out and the new one in. I knew that in front of the cathedral crowds would have gathered. That there'd be dancing, singing and drinking. I had never been allowed to go. Not even now that I was eighteen. 'A crowd of tinkers and gougers. Pissy-arsed drunks who'd as soon up with a bottle and split you open as wish you a Happy New Year,' my mother would say when I asked.

And as the last peal of bells rang out the dying year my mother's voice became mournful as she lamented all those she had known who had died in the one just gone, wondering how many of us would be alive to see the end of the year that was now being rung in. Her morbid fears were contagious. And I'd wonder if I'd be amongst the ones she'd be lamenting in twelve months' time.

I hated what I considered the Irish obsession with death. For as I long as I could remember I had looked at dead bodies. Brought to wakes by my mother. Paying ha'pennies to the sisters of the dead being waked in their homes. Sneaking into the dead house in the hospice to thrill and terrify myself. Walking the Dublin streets where so many hall-doors were festooned with black crêpe bows. Knowing that behind each lay a body surrounded by candles, crosses, Holy Water, covered mirrors and praying friends and relatives keeping their watch on the dead. Living in a street which was the main thoroughfare to Mount Jerome Cemetery. Where funerals proceeded one after the other. So many that your right arm suffered a temporary paralysis from making Signs of the Cross as the cortège passed.

And so for me New Year's Eve was another depressing experience. Not so for my mother. Once back in the house her ebullient spirit soared. Her voice rose in song. Usually 'I saw the old homestead, the faces I knew / I saw England's valleys and dells / And I listened with joy as I did when a boy to the sound of the old village bells!' As she sang she made ham sandwiches and wet tea. She had paid her homage to the dead. Now it was eat, drink and be merry.

England was so different. In the time I'd been there no one in the camp had been seriously ill. No one had died. I never saw or heard of a funeral. And the men I knew had cheated death. They were whole, handsome, alive and kicking.

England was glorious. Living without sorrow. Glorying in glorious health. Without ache or pain surrounded by others equally in exuberant health. So much energy coursing through you you wanted to run instead of walk, jump, turn cartwheels, dance. And always be in love.

As I was with Steve, who asked me to marry him. After he was demobilized, after he had been to university. But soon we would become engaged. I was ecstatic. Every girl I knew hoped for marriage. For an engagement ring. To be married in a white dress and veil. To be saved from the shelf, the slur of being an old maid.

We continued to find sheltered porches until the weather improved, and when it did we climbed down to the place of trees I had seen on my first day in camp. We found places where carpet upon carpet of leaves had escaped the rain. Where we lay and kissed. And where time and time again I stilled Steve's hand when it began wandering. For though I loved him and chastity was fading from my conscience, the fear of pregnancy was as real as ever. Pregnancy and my mother's warning that once you let a man have his way with you his respect was lost. You were less than the dirt beneath his feet. And he'd boast of his conquest. Tell his mates you were an easy mark. We'd smoke. We'd rise and walk through the woods admiring primroses and bluebells. Sometimes as an added precaution I took with me on our outings the blonde, beautiful three-year-old daughter of my friends in married quarters.

Eventually I allowed him one liberty. Ignoring the advice of my Jewish neighbour I let him touch me below the neck, place his hand over my left breast pocket, protected as it was by layers of thick khaki and the AB64 Part Two pay-book in its stiff canvas cover. For all the sensation he might as well have been caressing the sole of my shoe.

* * *

During 1946 men and women who had been conscripted at the beginning of the war were nearing their demobilization dates. The majority of the women came from disbanded anti-aircraft batteries. Some had manned the guns alongside the men. Quiet, friendly women, tired no doubt after their long ordeal. Several women serving with anti-aircraft batteries had been killed. Generally they didn't frequent the cafés or canteen. Many were married, some waiting to go up to university.

ATS drivers from redundant units were also posted in. They usually wore trousers, leather jerkins over their tunics and, almost permanently, their caps. I'd seen them get into bed still wearing the soft flat cap with its leather strap worn across the cap's top.

The men who were posted in swelled the ranks. From amongst so many there wasn't a girl, be she bandy, boss-arsed, cross-eyed or buck-toothed, who couldn't have got a man. Some, like Connie from Manchester, chose not to. She continued to read her socialist literature and castigate capitalism. Often she talked to me about the inequalities in society. I pretended to listen. Pretended to read the books and pamphlets she lent me. Despite her brusque, cynical manner and scathing comments when girls were broken-hearted over a failed romance, I liked her, her generosity and caustic wit.

The men were buoyed up with the thought of becoming civilians. Laughing and mocking about the prospective 'demob' suits, generally double-breasted and chalk-striped with a choice of trilby. They talked. Some of returning to the office, factory or whatever their pre-war occupation had been. Others were going for further education. Still others had grandiose plans to start a business, from which they hoped to make fortunes but more importantly to be their own boss.

* * *

Two new girls were assigned to our barrack room. Both, like me, were still in their teens. Kirsty was Scottish. Very shy. Friendly but reserved. Went to bed long before anyone else, got up early and had cleaned her bed space while we still slept. And refused invitations to the demob parties which came about regularly.

The other was a tall mournful-faced girl called Janetta. Her eyes were big and brown with a cow-like expression. Though not a live wire she joined in everything and was well liked.

Along with two other new arrivals Kirsty and Janetta were assigned to the switchboard. There were now six operators. We worked two-hourly shifts.

So much leisure. So many pleasurable ways in which to spend it. With Steve, if his off-duty coincided with mine. Walking along the banks of the neglected Basingstoke canal, its hedges entwined with honeysuckle, its heady sweetness inhaled with every breath. White and yellow water-lilies. Jewel-winged dragonflies skimming along the water. And on late summer evenings the hedge alight with glow-worms.

I had time to read. To write letters to Bubbles, Edith and Marj. Bubbles was waiting for a passage as a GI bride. Edith and Marj's letters were short on information but they wrote that they were well and happy.

Except on inspection mornings I could sleep late when not on first duty. Sleep in the afternoon. Attempt to swim in the scummy pool. Try my hand at tennis. Or walk to the village and join a crowd of men I was friendly with. Flirt with them and, though sometimes tempted, refuse dates. I was in love with Steve: one day we were going to become engaged.

Sometimes I chose to visit my friend in Married Quarters. If my hair needed trimming she trimmed it. Taught me how to apply nail varnish. Three strokes-a-broad, one to the centre of the nail and another to either side.

In her home I tasted home-made lemon meringue pie for the first time and learned that it was ill-mannered to ask for brown bottled sauce when your hostess had prepared delicious gravy to serve with the roast dinner. I defended myself. 'But we don't have gravy with our dinner in Ireland.'

'You're not in Ireland now,' she replied, and offered me the sauce boat.

* * *

Breda's American aunt sent her a parcel. Among its contents were two Maidenform brassières. 'Try one on,' Katy and I urged. Breda turned her back on us, took off her shirt and vest.

She wore a vest except in a heatwave. And put on the bra. 'Don't put that thing on,' said Katy, confiscating the vest, 'only your shirt. Now turn round.'

When she did Katy exclaimed, 'God, it's unbelievable. Lana Turner no less. The sweater girl herself.' Breda blushed and giggled. The transformation was amazing. Gone was the lumpy appendage that had fronted her chest, replaced by two pleasingly separated breasts almost on a level with her armpits.

'You look smashing, Breda. I wouldn't have thought a bra could make such a difference. Go and look in the mirror. Hang on,' Katy said and rummaged in her locker. 'Take off the shirt and try this.' It was her special sweater. Shetland, fine and the colour of cream.

Breda looked terrific in it. Other girls came to look and admire. 'Turn sideways, now the other side,' Katy ordered. Breda's face was the colour of beetroot.

'Are you sure they're not too, you know, too prominent? Immodest, like.' Katy threw the shirt at her and laughed. Gradually the blushes subsided, smiles replacing them. You could see Breda beginning to admire herself.

Every girl in the barrack room wanted a Maidenform. Army issue, we all agreed, were useless. One girl wondered aloud if you could get one in England. Maybe London, another suggested. But they'd cost a fortune apart from clothing coupons.

I made up my mind I would have a decent bra. I didn't need one with as much uplift as Breda's. My breasts weren't pendulous. I'd try Camberley. Wealthy people lived in Camberley. Shops there stocked items not available in Aldershot or Woking. I'd save money. Sell half of my fag ration. Not buy my sweet ration. And, something I'd never done before, sell my clothing coupons. Clothes rationing was non-existent in Dublin.

* * *

Katy and I often talked late into the night. Especially if she had been out on a date. Sometimes she reported in at the required time then pushed a pillow down in her bed to fool the duty corporal who often, but not always, came to stand at the barrack-room door and flash her torch along the beds. Katy would be long gone out the back way.

After one such episode she came to my bed asking if I was

awake. She was laughing. 'Ssh,' I whispered, 'you'll wake everyone.' I think she'd had a drink. Probably half a cider.

'You've got to hear this. You know I went out with a Canadian tonight. Well ...' She was a great mimic. Able to imitate almost any accent. Now she spoke like the bloke from Saskatchewan telling her of his war experiences. The Dieppe raid. His home town. All the small talk of a first date as they ate their pie and chips before finding somewhere to have a necking session.

Reverting to her Scottish accent she said, 'We went into that little wood by your church. He could kiss. Smelled OK. Then he got all worked up. Let go of me and started fumbling with his trousers. And the next thing,' she was back with the Canadian accent, 'he said, "Hold this." "What?" I asked. "This." He caught hold of my hand. I looked down and there was this enormous monster of a prick pointing at my belly button. "Please," he said, panting as if he'd run a mile.'

'And did you?'

'Like hell I did. "Hold it yourself," I said. "It looks too heavy." And I went quick. Leaving him standing. Dirty sod.'

On another night she told me another story about another Canadian. 'He was OK. We were stationed in Aldershot. I knew him for three months. Nothing special to look at. He was dark and on the thin side, not much taller than me. You'd pass him in the street without a second glance.'

Every so often during the telling she'd pause to drag deeply on her cigarette. Its tip glowed in the darkness of the barrack room.

'I'd just finished my Basic. I met him the first day I was posted to Aldershot. It was the end of May. Aldershot was packed with troops. Commandos, Canadians, everyone in the British army so it seemed. Anyway I met him in a Sally Anne canteen. The chestnut trees on Queens Avenue were in bloom. Hundreds of trees with all these pinky white candles. Beautiful.

'Then the rumours began. No one knew for sure but everyone guessed something was in the air. There were so many wild guesses. Such an air of expectancy. And then one night the sound of marching feet. I knew, all the girls in the barrack room knew, it had to be the Canadians. Their barracks were the nearest to ours. They'd gone to Dieppe. A few days afterwards the news broke. The Canadian casualties were terrible. I kept hoping that maybe he'd been taken prisoner. But he'd have written.'

'So you never knew for sure?'

'No, never.'

The next morning Katy was her usual flip self and never again mentioned her Canadian sweetheart. But our storytelling continued periodically. Usually with me as the narrator. 'Tell us one of your Irish stories,' one of the girls would say on a night when for some reason or another a few of us were still awake after lights out. And I'd tell of the Banshee. Imitate the keen she was supposed to wail. How she sat combing her grey hair. The danger you courted by approaching her. For then she'd throw the comb at you and during the week you or one of your family was certain to die.

I told of the changelings. Ugly, grizzled fairy children swapped during the night for the plump, rosy-cheeked infant put to bed by their adoring mothers who on waking found in its place the puny mewling fairy child. And I explained the reason. D'ye see, the mother or father would have displeased the little people.'

'How?' someone would ask.

I invented as I went along. 'Maybe they hadn't left a saucer of milk out for them and they thirsty. Or might have said, "Wisha sure, seeing is believing and in all my born days I've never laid eyes on a fairy."'

I embellished and exaggerated, enjoying the sound of my own voice. One night I excelled myself and was so carried away by my narration that for a while I didn't realize I was the only one left awake. The helmets and rolled-up groundsheets hanging from pegs above the facing beds assumed terrifying shapes. Grinning skulls and limbless bodies. Visions of the hospice wards and emaciated faces. The arch above the gates which spelled out the fate awaiting the sick who passed beneath them. 'Our Lady's Hospice for the Dying'. I saw again the mortuary chapel and the body of my father on his marble slab. And then I heard his voice. Good-naturedly mocking my mother as she related her story of the Banshee and her keening. 'Courting cats.' And to myself I smiled. And remembered him as he was. My lovely, joyous father. The thudding of my heart subsided and when I looked again at the helmets and groundsheets I saw that that was all they were.

THIRTEEN

'**D**on't go yet, Private Bolger,' the voice of the physical training instructor halted my rush to the gymnasium door.

As always during the training period I had been vigorous, supple, eager to impress her with my aptitude for exercise and activity. She stood, smiling, winding a skipping rope round its handles. Her shorts were short, her white aertex shirt immaculate and, although it was early May, her skin already tanned.

'I've been watching you for a while. You're good. It's obvious you enjoy the lessons.'

'I love them.'

'Have you ever thought of being a PTI?'

'Always. From my very first lesson.'

'Would you like me to put your name forward for a course?'

I was suffused with joy. At last my dream was about to come true. Many times I despaired of the call. Now it had come.

'Would that mean I'd be like you? A full corporal?' Through my mind flew visions of snowy lanyards and silvery whistles. Shorts made to fit. Sports shirts, extra money to up my mother's allowance.

'No,' she said, 'not at first.' The dreams tumbled about my feet.

'If you're accepted and pass the course you'd be a part-time instructor. Take classes when I'm not available. As you know, I cover a large area and don't always get to this camp on a regular basis.'

'Oh,' I said. 'And the track suit and all the things you wear?'

'I'm afraid not. They are only issued to full-time instructors.'

'But the promotion, I'd get that?'

'Only after becoming a full-time instructor, then you'd get

two stripes. I suppose you are aware that if you were eventually made up to full corporal it would mean a posting out of here?'

I had a lump in my throat. My dream shattered. No posh kit. No elevated rank. And if one day I did become a full-time instructor I'd be posted out. Away from all I loved. Steve. My friends. This lovely place. What good would two stripes and a track suit be amongst strangers? It wasn't fair. I'd been tricked into believing something that wasn't true.

My heart dropped. Misery must have been apparent on my face. For the instructor said in a consoling voice, 'Cheer up. Don't look so disappointed. I'm sure you'd do very well on the course. And by this time next year you'd get the full-time one. In the long run the choice is yours. Don't decide now. We'll talk about it again next week. You'd better go or you'll miss break-fast.'

I slouched back to the billet, my hunger gone. The thought of bread and margarine with steamed fish or dried egg made me feel nauseated. I wasn't on duty until after lunch. I'd go back to bed. Go to sleep. Feel sorry for myself. If the Company Sergeant-Major should come into the barrack room and ask why I wasn't up, I'd lie. Say I had a headache. Period pains. I hugged my misery and was about to drop off when I heard Sylvia's voice.

Sylvia had recently been posted in. She was years older than me, a conscript who was now on a long-term engagement. A corporal in the clothing stores who had attached herself to us. She was extraordinarily generous. Treating us to suppers if we weren't dating. Tea, coffee and cakes at break time. Imitation Bakewell tarts made with semolina in place of ground almonds. Banana sandwiches which consisted of parsnips flavoured with the fruit's essence. She lent us money and flashed her fags around.

'I dropped in to see if anyone was about. What's the matter with you?' She sat on the side of my bed while I sobbed out my story. 'You daft ha'porth. Here. Sit up.' She put a pillow behind me. 'Anyone would think you'd been turned down. You go on the course. You'll walk through it. You're good. I've watched you. You won a medal for the hundred yards last year. You're a reserve for Southern Command netball team. The stuff PTIs are made of. But you've got to have patience. One step at a time. That's how it is in the army. Next year you'll be full-time. A corporal. I'll buy your stripes and stitch them on for you.'

'But then I'll be posted out.' There was still a catch in my voice. 'Have to leave you all, and Steve.'

'That's what the army's about—moving on. And Steve will be gone himself by then. Now, get up and get dressed. It's Thursday—deep-fried jam butties.'

I looked at her coarse-featured face. She was so good, so kind. And I felt guilty for all the times Katy, Breda and I, while mumping from her, laughed not with her but at her. Katy said she had a face like a potato, reminding us of the celluloid noses, mouths and pairs of eyes we'd had as children to stick into potatoes. Cynical Katy also said Sylvia bought our friendship, for who else would listen to her tall stories? Her refusal to use the swimming pool was because the diving board wasn't high enough. Her serve was too powerful to play tennis with us. But it was the story of her life that had Katy tearing her hair out.

According to Sylvia, her mother had been a great beauty. A poor girl, reared over a tripe shop in Accrington. She ran away from home. In London she met a young Hussar. They fell in love. His family was fabulously wealthy. Fortuitously they were killed in a car accident. The Hussar inherited their fortune. Married Sylvia's mother, went with his regiment to India where Sylvia was born. Where she lived until she was seven. She described her ayah, tiger shoots, pig sticking, monsoons, her pet elephant, muezzins, vultures, dhobis. Going up into the Hills in the hot season.

Then tragedy struck. Her father was eaten by a tiger. Her mother inherited the fortune, and set off by the longest route back to England. Changed ship many times. Disembarked anywhere there was a casino and arrived in England penniless.

Back to Accrington and the tripe shop. Where her granny was less than welcoming. And her mother died of a fever, caused, Sylvia said, by the chitterlings, pigs' feet, sheets of tripe and buckets of blood for making black puddings which went off in the summer.

As soon as she was old enough Sylvia ran away to work in a hotel. In Blackpool she got a job as a cocktail waitress and there met Hutch, the famous black singer. He fell madly in love with her, and bought her an engagement ring so valuable she never wore it. It was kept in a display case in the opulent foyer.

At this point in the story Sylvia would look at her watch, gasp, and announce she had forgotten she was meeting someone. One

of her mysterious admirers. All of them officers whom she enter-
tained in her room. She had one attached to the clothing store.

We never met any of her admirers, but we were shown the
gifts they gave her. Silk scarves, scent and expensive soaps,
creams and toiletries.

When she talked about Daddy and India she had 'the voice',
but for everyday she spoke with a Lancashire accent.

As I dressed I thought how she was what would be described
as a fine lump of a woman in Ireland. Big and tall. A great help
on a small farm.

She had beautiful eyes. Blue like a delft plate and they were
seldom without a smile. She never said a malicious word about
anyone. And encouraged us to beware of men's promises. Never
to bestow our favours lightly.

* * *

In the NAFFI while eating our deep-fried jam butties Sylvia
asked, 'Are you coming to the dance on Friday?'

'If Steve will. Are you?'

'I wouldn't miss it for the world. It's a dress affair.'

The voice came into play after I'd asked, 'A dress affair.
What's that?'

'The officers will wear Number One dress and their wives
will beg, borrow or steal a ball gown. This is one of the first
dress affairs since the war. I finished mine last night.'

Katy would have loved what followed; it would have confirmed her belief that Sylvia was a lunatic. 'It's fabulous. Black,
floaty and I've ordered a pale pink orchid from Camberley.'

I was impressed. 'You must have been saving or buying
coupons from that spiv.'

'Not on your nelly.' Her northern accent was back.
'Mosquito netting. Yards and yards of it. I dyed it black. The
skirt has three layers.'

I nearly choked on the last mouthful of jam butty. She had a
machine. She could sew but knew as much about style as I did
about mathematics. I was familiar with her creations.

She had three suits. Black, nigger brown and navy blue.
Made from surplus ATS uniforms which she had dyed, replaced
the brass buttons and trimmed every available space with matching silk fringe. They looked what they were, badly dyed ATS

uniforms. With the black and navy ones she wore a large-brimmed hat in vivid red and with the brown a canary-yellow beret.

Many times when wearing the red hat, she told us, she had been mistaken for Rosalind Russell, and Marlene Dietrich when wearing the beret. With that she didn't agree. 'Rosalind, yes, we are the same build and colouring. How people can compare me with Marlene I don't understand.'

'I'll definitely go to the dance,' I told her as we finished coffee and lit up. 'Whether Steve comes or not.' Not for anything in the world would I miss the woman in black make her entrance.

'Then come with me on Friday afternoon to pick up my orchid.'

'OK. Maybe I could get a bra at the same time. But I'm short of …'

'Money?' Sylvia asked.

'I have enough money. I've been saving. No, it's coupons.'

'Not to worry, cock, I've loads of coupons.'

So on the following Friday we went by bus to Camberley. Before setting off I saw her ball gown. She tried it on. Three layers of skirts. Soft lifeless netting which clung to her legs and bum. 'There's so much fullness,' she said, 'I won't need an underskirt.'

The dye had taken unevenly. It resembled smoke from a variety of fuels. Patchy black as if from a conflagration of rubber, and ashy grey as if damp peat had been burned.

I could have worn my lovely coat, nylons and a pair of court shoes a relation had given me. But I knew that Sylvia preferred me to dress casually. She told me casual clothes suited me. Maybe they did. Maybe she didn't want competition, for she was wearing her black suit and large red hat. I wore a pair of scruffy corduroy trousers with a beautiful pure fine wool blouse in green and blue checks, a gift from the giver of the court shoes.

Sylvia told me I looked like Huckleberry Finn and mentioned again her resemblance to Rosalind. I was embarrassed for her but consoled myself that as far as she was concerned she was a 'knockout' and that was what mattered.

The nearer we got to Camberley the more she used 'the voice'. Talking loudly. Sometimes lapsing for seconds into her

Lancashire accent. Hitting her G endings too hard and saying uz instead of us.

She knew which shop sold lingerie, and I soon owned two Kestos brassières. Frail, pale pink cotton cups with an elastic arrangement which fastened by loops to buttons beneath each breast. Examining them in the shop I was doubtful they would give me the line which Breda's Maidenform had. 'Try them on. You should never buy foundation garments without trying them on,' the assistant advised.

I did. 'And now your shirt,' said Sylvia. 'You can't judge properly without a sweater or blouse.' I put on my shirt and viewed myself sideways. My breasts were uplifted, pointed, my nipples prominent. I told the assistant I'd keep it on, and walked through Camberley streets as sure as Sylvia was of the impression she made that I was getting my share of attention. I imagined the effect when I would wear the bra beneath my longed-for aertex sports shirt. (When eventually I did I was banned from crossing the square when officer cadets were on parade. The Commanding Officer passed word to the ATS CO that I had a distracting effect on his men.)

Sylvia pointed out the Staff College, where the cream of the British army was commissioned, and explained how on passing-out parades the adjutant rode his white horse up the college steps.

We left collecting the orchid until the last minute. Going beforehand to a café called, I think, The Copper Kettle. A genteel woman in a floral smock brought a cake-stand of home-made scones, two tiny pats of butter and a small bowl of quince jam. The clientele was mostly middle-aged women, a sprinkling of officers and cadets. Sylvia talked loudly and then brayed a laugh. People stared. Lowering her voice and smiling, she said, 'They've noticed the resemblance. Everywhere I go the same thing happens.'

I was too engrossed in wolfing down scones to feel embarrassed for her. Later on that night at the ball I did. I could have cried for her as she paraded round in the hideous dress. Approaching and engaging in conversation with officers and their wives who politely snubbed her. Warrant Officers with whom I had seen her flirt flagrantly shunning her because they were accompanied by their wives. No one asked her to dance. The pale pink orchid drooped.

I had gin. Neat gin. I had two. I don't remember who bought them for me. Their effect was startling. Suddenly I wanted to be with Steve in our sheltered porch. But he was in deep conversation with another soldier who was going to read medicine. By the time he was ready to take me to the billet or porch the effect of the gin had worn off. I was sad and depressed, having seen Sylvia leave the gymnasium and return after a little while wearing a royal blue, blanket-cloth dressing-gown. 'I didn't have a wrap,' she said, 'and I was freezing so I put this on.'

FOURTEEN

At last I was about to assume the glamorous role I had envisaged from my first days in basic training. On the Company Notice Board were the details. My name, rank and number. To report to Hammersley Barracks, School of Physical Training, Aldershot, for a course as a part-time instructor.

* * *

The cheerless barrack room, a group of strangers, everyone new and inexperienced, reminded me of when I joined up. But, as in training centre, we soon made friends.

For the first few days we rose from our beds like arthritic old women. Backs, knees, ankles, shoulders, calves, feet—wherever there was a joint or muscle unaccustomed to strenuous exercise, it ached.

Gradually we loosened up. Became supple. Were taught how to instruct. How to referee certain games. Correct poor posture. Recognize flat feet and set exercises to correct them. Our toes remembered their prehensile function, grasped marbles, lifted and shifted them. A cure for fallen arches, we were assured.

We attended lectures on hygiene. How to avoid verrucas by avoiding wooden duckboards. Lectures on the beneficial effects of regular exercise, on the bowel, bladder, heart, liver and lungs. We took copious notes. Asked and answered questions, ambitious girls like me drawing attention to themselves. Hands up. Questioning. Answering. In the spotlight, initiative being a virtue in the army.

There were girls as agile as monkeys who in breaks between lessons did handstands, cartwheeled for yards across the gymnasium and shinned up and down ropes as if they'd served their time on sailing ships. Not me. Fortunately acrobatic skills were not part of the course requirements and I passed with flying colours. The result was forwarded to my company along with a recommendation for a course as a full-time instructor and promotion to the rank of corporal when a vacancy occurred.

I was halfway there. Every time I passed the village shop selling stripes and crossed swords, the emblem of the School of Physical Training which I'd wear above my stripes, I was tempted to buy them. But being Irish and superstitious I resisted. It wasn't wise to spit in the wind.

I thought of the extra money, making my mother's allowance up to ten shillings a week. Though now the need was no longer pressing. She had a job, as a seamstress with the Irish army. My brother joined the RAF and made her a generous allowance and soon my sister would be leaving school and had a job lined up.

She was 'on the pig's back', my mother, or almost. For there was still a house to acquire. We only had two rooms. Upstairs were two other tenants. My mother was very fond of one of them, a middle-aged laundry worker who smoked millions of cigarettes and liked a few bottles of stout. Her face was leathery and brown. Cured like a kipper by tobacco. And from out of the wrecked face shone a pair of enormous brown eyes with always a beautiful smile in them.

She was pro-British. On her way in from the public house she would knock on our kitchen door, come in and regale us with songs of the First World War. In her cracked, hoarse voice she sang 'Roses Are Shining in Picardy', 'Tipperary', 'There's a Long, Long Road a-Winding' and countless others until a fit of coughing overwhelmed her.

The other tenant was young, married and had three children. My mother didn't object to the children nor the commandeering of the washing line. But when the pig appeared she declared war. Its sty was underneath our kitchen window. Buckets of greasy cabbage water and basins of vegetable peelings were delivered to the door, causing my mother to foam at the mouth.

The young woman fought her corner, defending her 'little pig's right to nourishment'. The war raged for months. The stench in the yard was noxious.

My mother was tearing her hair out. 'A pig in the yard and

next door a shaggin' chicken butcher. No wonder the place is infested with rats.'

'Don't forget the cats,' said my brother, who sat by the window, catapult in hand, taking aim at the constant trail of cats padding along the back wall to feast on the innards of the slaughtered chickens. 'Got him,' he'd whoop with glee when his shot found its target.

Between the constant rows and my mother's complaints to the Department of Health, the woman with the pig moved to a Corporation house. My mother scoured the yard with buckets of scalding water laced with washing soda and had a word with the landlord, a giant of a man who'd thrown the hammer or discus at a long-ago Olympic Games. He did his own repairs, putting the heart crossways in my mother when it was the roof that needed mending. She prayed fervently. Not necessarily for his safety, but that if it was God's will that he should fall, let it be anywhere but through the roof.

He let my mother have the vacant room. Sadly she soon had possession of the other one. Jessie, the laundry worker, got severe bronchitis and went into heart failure. While waiting for the priest and doctor my mother sat by the bed, holding her hand and whispering to her the Act of Contrition.

She mourned Jessie. We all did. Nevertheless we welcomed the extra room. My mother blossomed, for at last she had achieved her two ambitions.

* * *

Breda's chic hairstyle and uplifted breasts belied the sweet naïve girl she still was. One night when Steve was on guard duty she and I went to the NAFFI for supper. It was Thursday, not the best night to choose. Thursday was pay day and soldiers who didn't fancy the walk to the village drank there.

We found a table that wasn't too littered with empty cigarette packets and overflowing ashtrays and spilt tea, coffee and beer. The coffee was as usual foul, the chips welded together with grease and the pie a lucky dip. Being young, healthy and ravenous we began eating.

A soldier played the piano. He was good. I loved 'Stardust' and listened. He changed his tune to 'Bless 'em All', to which the crowd gathered round him sang the words, 'Sod 'em All'.

Not very offensive. But Breda's standards were high. She turned to glare. Although in their state of intoxication it would have been lost on the sweaty-faced, bleary-eyed men. Then she exclaimed in a horrified voice, 'Will you look at that!'

'What? Where?' I asked.

'Around the piano.'

I turned to look. Saw nothing out of the ordinary. Turning back I said, 'It's pay day. Someone's always drunk on Thursday night.'

'I know that but this is different.'

'Why?' I asked, undoing my lucky dip which appeared to be filled only with burnt onions.

'Because they're Pioneers.'

'So they're in the Pioneer Corps.'

'I know that but they're not supposed to drink.'

'Since when?'

'Are you trying to be funny? You're Irish. You know well Pioneers don't drink. They've all taken the Pledge. Drink mustn't pass their lips.'

'You're not serious?'

'Of course I am.'

I laughed out loud and couldn't stop for a few minutes.

'There's nothing to laugh at,' Breda said as huffily as she could manage.

I controlled my laughter. Well, almost. Then enlightened her. 'Breda, Pioneers in the British Army, most of them anyway, are manual labourers. They dig ditches and drains. Do the rough work. They can get stocious every night of the week. Legless, so long as they dig the following day. They know nothing about the Pledge. Maybe a few who are Irish may have heard of it. But they've absolutely nothing to do with any abstinence movement.'

'Honest to God?'

'Honest to God.'

'Well, amn't I the right eejit.'

You are, I thought, but the nicest eejit I've ever known. And I want to be your friend all my life.

I couldn't wait to get back to the billet and tell Katy.

* * *

I stood in for the PT Corporal on mornings when she couldn't attend. On the first occasion I was nervous. But after that I revelled in taking classes. The clerical staff exercised before breakfast, mumbling and grumbling, only half awake. But the majority came to and before the lesson ended showed signs of enjoying it. When on duty, cooks and orderlies were up at dawn, and when on their rest days or late shift they had PT later in the morning. I would go to their barrack room to rouse them and warn that the lesson would begin in half an hour. Once on a bright summer's morning, invigorated after the earlier session, I bent over an orderly, touching her gently awake. A young girl wearing her khaki turban under which I could see the shapes of her curlers. She was snoring softly. I bent again to rouse her and then recoiled in horror. Her face was crawling with lice. I had seen lice before, on the faces of corpses. Seen them tumble from heads including my own, raked out before the teeth of a fine comb. But never on the face of a living person. My stomach churned. I went out to breathe fresh air and calm myself. My skin crawled. I lit a cigarette while deciding what to do.

Reluctant to report her, then realizing there was nothing else I could do, I went to the Company Sergeant-Major's office. Miss Long was a diminutive Scotswoman. Silver-haired, quick moving. She reminded me of a fox terrier. The welfare of her girls, she constantly reminded us, was her great concern.

Many times at night I had seen her, torch in hand, wandering through the camp keeping an eye on her girls. Katy and I often warned Sylvia that one night Miss Long might pay a visit while Sylvia was entertaining the men she boasted visited her.

I reported the girl with lice. 'Come with me,' Miss Lang said. It was an order. I led the way. The girl was still sleeping, the lice crawling. Miss Long shook her roughly, ordered her to dress, not remove the turban and report to the medical inspection room. She dismissed me with a 'Thank you'. I flew to the NAFFI. Only Katy and Sylvia were there. Neither was squeamish. They listened while eating doughnuts, though both began to scratch. Katy finished eating, then exclaimed, 'Yesterday she served my dinner.'

Sylvia shuddered. 'Mine too. The stew was probably swimming with them.'

We rubbed our backs against the chairs trying to relieve the imaginary itching.

'You know, if there's a dance or a date coming up some orderlies keep their curlers in for days. Wearing turbans all the time they get away with it,' Katy said.

'Not anymore they won't. There'll be head inspections left, right and centre. Miss Long will see to that.'

Katy went to get more coffee and Sylvia continued talking. 'Their hair wouldn't see brush or comb for days on end. What a ball the lice would have had.'

When Katy came back she had news of the orderly. 'I've just been talking to Vera from the MI Room. Guess what?'

We couldn't. She enlightened us. 'They set about delousing her. Made her take out the curlers and discovered she has septic dermatitis. She's being sent to hospital this afternoon. Hind-head in Surrey. And along with treatment she's to have her head shaved.'

'God, I wonder how many more there are like her? I'm not going to the cookhouse until the head inspections have been done. Can you believe it—in that condition serving our food.' I felt sick. I kept seeing what I'd seen when I pulled the sheets and blankets from the girl's face.

Later we heard that the orderly, after being discharged from hospital, was sent home on sick leave. Until her hair grew, we assumed. She didn't return to the camp. And the head inspections found no one heavily infested. We began eating in the cookhouse again. Lack of money forced us to.

* * *

I became more confident taking the PT lessons. Confident and conscientious, spending part of evenings preparing the follow-ing day's lesson, though occasionally if I'd had a late night I'd take the lazy way out and order 'a run'. Once out of sight of places where Miss Long might spy us I slowed down the pace, so that until we neared the camp again it had become a walk. I got on well with male instructors and, though strictly speaking the gymnasium was their territory, I was free to wander in and out at any time. They flirted and teased in a pleasant way. Dis-played their superb bodies. The gymnasium smelled of their clean sweat, which I liked. Vaguely aware that it was disturbing. Sexually, I know now.

I liked watching them working on the parallel bars, vaulting over the horse, practising complicated turns and twists. One, a wiry, low-sized Geordie, I remember balancing on the horse, his body straight as an arrow supported only by his little finger. Years later, long after I had left the forces, I saw him again, on television, performing the same feat.

But as is the case amongst any group of people there was a horror. Sandy, a cock of the walk. An ex-miner from Nottingham. Ugly, but a fabulous body. Within my hearing he boasted of his conquests, more than implying what a gift he was to women. Lewdly winking at me. I pretended not to hear or notice. But once I did overhear a remark of his. He was swinging on a rope and shouted to another PTI working out on the mat, 'Last time for the one I had last night, Jack.'

'How's that?'

'Like shoving your arm up a bloody flue it were,' Sandy replied.

Katy told me what it meant and went on to say, 'She was lucky he didn't put the ferret up.'

'The ferret?'

'Didn't you know he goes ferreting? Supposed to carry it around in his trousers.'

FIFTEEN

Steve's date of demobilization was drawing near. End of August. He'd be out in time to go to medical school in the autumn. The following spring we'd get engaged. On my way to Dublin I'd break the journey at Crewe where he, having travelled down from Glasgow, would meet me in the middle of the night. Next day we'd choose the ring.

The thought of possessing an engagement ring occupied my thoughts. It was a status symbol. I remembered from the factory how we'd gather round newly engaged girls to admire their minuscule diamonds. Envious and hoping for the day when we had one to display. But thoughts of the commitment involved in this status worried me. Six long years with no dates. Only occasionally seeing Steve. We couldn't afford to marry until he qualified. Six years. An eternity. No kissing and loving except when we'd briefly meet. Not that often. Neither of us had money for long train journeys.

A long, lonely time. Engaged girls didn't date. They stayed in in the evenings. Saved for their wedding. Not such a hardship for civilians living at home, usually in the same vicinity as their fiancé. Not so easy to cope with in the forces, where you were surrounded by attractive men. Where apart from sitting on your bed there was only the recreation room. And for most of the week not a cup of tea or slice of bread between the last canteen meal and breakfast the next morning. For you wouldn't have a date to pay your way.

Sometimes I'd fantasize. When Steve and I met at Crewe we'd elope. Go to Gretna Green and marry. I'd get my discharge. Find work in Glasgow. Find a room where we could live. My money would help him through college. The fantasy didn't last long. Steve, though in the army labelled as unreliable and a tearaway, was determined to make a success of his medical career. He lived at home. His family weren't poor. He didn't need me to help pay his way. Nor would he, I believed, want to take me into a slum bedsit. One of his ambitions was to have me live in comfort when he was a doctor.

I loved him. I really did. I'd be devastated when he went. We'd write. And I consoled myself that my sentence in purdah didn't have to begin until I was wearing his ring. When I wasn't on duty I could still go to my favourite café, meet the boys and play dice for milkshakes. I never had to buy the round when I lost.

Amongst the crowd was a newcomer. His name was Johnny. Physically he was the complete opposite of Steve. Shorter, though not by much. Very dark. His curly hair black and his eyes brown. His teeth were perfect and the whitest I'd ever seen. The only ethnic group I knew were Jews. I thought he might be Jewish. I knew several Jews with beautiful olive-coloured skin. Skin that appeared always suntanned. Johnny had that sort of skin. Sometimes our fingers touched and a shiver ran through me. A sensation like a shiver only it made me hot and cold. I knew he fancied me. But remembering Steve and our coming engagement, I didn't encourage Johnny.

* * *

Tomorrow Steve was going to Aldershot, from where he would be demobilized. Tonight was the party in the village public house. There was a 'kitty' for the drinks. But men who liked and admired Steve bought him drinks outside the round. He was toasted and ribbed. Clapped on the back and plied with whiskey, with which he chased his pints of beer. There was a sing-song. Then individuals were called on to sing solo.

Steve sang to me, 'I'll Be Loving You Always, Till the End of Time', and finished his repertoire with our favourite, 'My Love Is Like a Red, Red Rose'. I was euphoric. If we had been alone in a sheltered porch or on our carpet of leaves I'm convinced Steve could have done anything he liked with me. I felt sad and romantic. Tears ran down my face. He kissed them away. Breda cried. Connie rolled her eyes towards the ceiling. Sylvia recalled her love affair with 'Hutch'; Katy asked why she never wore the fabulous ring? Why she had never shown it to us? Why she and the singer hadn't married? Sylvia sobbed convincingly. 'It was the colour thing. I knew Mummy and Daddy wouldn't have approved,' she replied in her perfect imitation of 'the voice'.

Breda, the soberest of us, leant close to me and whispered, 'Sure according to her story they were dead by then.'

'Shut up,' I hissed. Sylvia was a liar. And I knew the old saying, 'A liar needs a good memory.' The drink had addled Sylvia's. Her lies were harmless. I liked her, felt sorry for her. She was pathetic in another of her dyed army uniform get-ups. The nigger-brown with a pillbox hat in matching colour and a veil pushed back over it to accommodate her long green cigarette holder.

Katy was like a terrier worrying a rat. 'So, what did you do with the ring, flog it, pawn it?'

'Katy! What a terrible thing to suggest. I did the honourable thing of course,' replied Sylvia, dabbing at her eyes with a wisp of lace-trimmed cambric. 'I gave it back.'

* * *

Passionately Steve and I clung to each other in a lecture-hut porch. With great urgency his hands began to wander. And when my knees were beginning to feel weak and great surges of exciting feelings coursed through me, his legs buckled and he fell to the ground.

I touched him and called his name. He lay still. He was dead, I thought, running from the porch screaming for help. Two soldiers, staggering, stumbling and singing were approaching.

'Quick, quick,' I shouted, 'I think Steve's dead.'

'Bloody hell, that's a rum do,' one said. 'Let's have a decko.'

They lurched towards the porch. Then I heard a familiar voice roar. Ginger's.

'What the bloody hell's going on?' I clung to him.

'It's Steve, he's dead. Oh my God what'll I do?'

The soberer of the soldiers said, 'Her bloke's kicked the bucket, Sarge. Straight up.'

'Get outta the way,' Ginger ordered. 'On the double.' He bent over Steve. 'Drunk,' he declared. 'Passed out. Warned you, didn't I, Pad.'

'Then he's not dead?'

'No. The useless sod's not dead. You,' he said to one of the soldiers. 'Gimme a hand to stand him up.' Steve was hoisted to his feet. I wanted to cradle him in my arms. And hated Ginger when he slapped him across the face, shook him roughly and roared for him to wake up. Steve muttered something unintelligible before falling asleep or passing out again.

Ginger and the soldier walked him out of the porch. 'You.' He pointed to the second soldier. 'Grab hold of his other arm. Hold him here until I come back. I'll walk you to your billet,' he said to me.

I was still crying. 'He's leaving at five in the morning. I won't see him to say goodbye,' I sobbed.

'Good riddance.'

'But he's going away for good. We'll be separated.'

'That breaks my heart. You're a little fool. That bloke's no good. The sooner you forget him the better. Good war record. Nothing else to recommend him.'

'He won't die, will he, I mean he won't die during the night?'

'Not unless he chokes on his vomit.'

'Oh, Ginger.'

'Don't worry, kid. I'll lock him up for the night. We'll keep an eye on him.' We reached my billet. 'And you take my advice, dump the Scottish git,' he said.

I believed I was broken-hearted. Breda and Sylvia tried comforting me. Not letting me get up for breakfast when I wasn't working. Bringing me cups of tea and slices of bread from the cookhouse. Carrying the enamel mug up the wooded slope of the plateau. They spoke kindly and listened to my endless protestations of loss and grief. Katy made it obvious that she felt I was overplaying my hand. She never said so in so many words, but I knew her so well I could interpret her every word and gesture. Her judgment was probably influenced by my going to the café when I had an afternoon free. On afternoons I knew Johnny would be there. But nevertheless, I truly believed my life had ended with Steve's departure. I was inconsolable until his letters began arriving.

He wrote pages and pages in his small, square handwriting. How much he missed me. How much he loved me. He wrote descriptions of me. A me I didn't recognize. A me of wondrous beauty. Soft, silky, sweet-smelling hair. A mouth that tasted gorgeous. My soft full lips. The smile that lit my face.

He imagined how I would look naked. How he would

stroke my body, worship it. He wrote that he thought of me all day and before he went to sleep willed himself to dream of me. He didn't always but when he did, he hated wakening and losing me.

My replies must have been disappointing, for although I missed him, his kisses, the sight, sound and scent of him, I could put none of it down on paper. I tried but on reading it back it didn't ring true. It didn't flow as his words did. So I settled for a few declarations of love and then wrote about the camp gossip.

How Miss Long had routed Marilyn and the post corporal in the middle of a Saturday afternoon. Knocked on the post room door and demanded entry. Looked in each room and finally in a cupboard, where a naked Marilyn crouched behind mail bags. I told him that while none of us liked Marilyn, we felt she'd been treated badly.

'Stripped and posted. And the creep only admonished.'

In another letter I wrote about Breda and her spiv. Reminding him of the many times he'd heard the story of Breda's mother's desperate need for oilcloth for the scullery. How Breda ranted and raved that with the war being over you'd think a bit of oilcloth wouldn't be hard to come by. How, on a date with the cockney spiv, he was told of her mother's predicament and offered a solution. If Breda let him feel her knee he'd get the oilcloth. How indignantly she related the tale to me and Katy. How hard we'd found it not to laugh. And then Breda's final comment before she went to have a bath: 'And in any case how could I have got a roll of oilcloth home to Southampton'— where her mother had recently rented a house. Me and Katy were convulsed with laughter.

I didn't mention playing dice in the café or how attentive Johnny was becoming. Instead I wrote that I was counting the days until we met at Crewe. That once Christmas was over the days would fly.

I also wrote that I was going to Brighton for New Year. Going to see my grandfather and a sister of my father's.

SIXTEEN

I expected a scathing letter from my mother when she got the news of the Brighton trip and word that I wouldn't be home until the spring. Instead she sent me a pound and told me to note everything about my father's relations, my grandfather in particular. To remember every word he said and let him know how much she thought of him. And remind him that my brother had been called after him. But not a word about him hating the name and only using it for official purposes.

My grandfather's name was Theodore. He had brothers called Nelson and Bowman, so I suppose my brother fared better than their sons if family Christian names prevailed. But Theodore was a great embarrassment in a country where every other boy was a Michael, Brendan, Bernard or Patrick. My mother chose the name in the hope that her father-in-law would remember his namesake in his will. This excuse or explanation was no consolation to my brother and I don't think he ever forgave my mother for so naming him.

* * *

One evening Katy, Breda, Sylvia and I were talking. They were doing most of it. My mind was miles away. Imagining how I'd be received by my father's people. The fuss my grandfather would make of me. I would be staying with my aunt in Brighton. She had, according to my father, the same beautiful hair as her mother. She'd talk to me about her mother. About my father. Remember incidents from their childhood. The holidays they had spent in Horsham. She'd make him seem alive again.

Katy's voice broke in on my meanderings. 'Did you hear what I was saying?' she asked.

'Bits,' I replied. 'Tell me again.'

'I was just saying how this time next year we'll all be gone.'

'Gone where?'

'Home. Edinburgh, Ireland, Southampton. Wherever we decide to settle. Demobbed. Out of the forces.'

Not me. She had mentioned Dublin. But Katy couldn't have meant me. It seemed only yesterday I had joined up. This doubt must have showed on my face. For Katy asked, 'What year did you join up in?'

'1945.'

'Next year's '47. You'll have served your time. You didn't think it'd last for ever? You didn't want it to, did you?'

Oh, but I did. Forever and ever. My paradise. My haven where no one got seriously ill. No one died. No one talked of death. Where everyone was young. My land of Tír na nÓg.

Where I watched the seasons change. Spring resurrect the trees. Deck them in green buds. Cover the branches in leaves. Hang pussy willows from them. Set horse chestnuts ablaze with pink and white candles. Litter the woods with bluebells and primroses. Hear the cuckoo. Wild flowers in abundance. Lacy-headed cow parsley. I was learning to identify flowering weeds. Such names: Dusky Cranesbill, Shepherd's Purse, Lady's Slipper, Nipplewort.

Later on rowan berries. Prickly podded sweet chestnut nested in their fleshy white wombs. Scarlet, white-spotted toadstools. Like pictures in a storybook. And the golden, yellow, russet leaves in my place of the trees. And the sky. The endless sky. On clear nights filled with stars and the face of the man in the moon. And when it snowed it stayed white as it had fallen. Lay on the branches of trees. Covered the cricket field, the ground each side of the slope down to the cookhouse. No, I didn't want to leave, didn't want to go home, back to a factory treading a machine. I wanted to stay. Stay where grown-up girls played games. Bathed six times a day if they wanted to. Had six pairs of knickers, unglamorous though they might be. Where white sheets and towels were laundered once a week.

I was devastated. How had time flown so quickly? Why hadn't I been aware that it had? Because I had been so happy. Every moment filled with pleasure. Pleasure I was constantly aware of. Surrounded by attractive, adoring men. Aware that I had blossomed. Being in love. Being loved in return.

No mother prying, preaching, probing. I couldn't go back. Not to a factory. To compulsory mass. Chapels where you paid your entrance. A penny for the body where the poor sat. Almost all in shabby clothes. Some in dirty ones. Watch the lice weave in and out of their hair. Farting men who'd drunk too much the previous night, the smell of their foul wind wafting around mixed with burning grease of candles, incense and the sour breath from stomachs fasting from the night before so they could receive Communion. While in the threepenny and six-penny places sat powdered women swathed in sealskin and musquash. Men in pressed suits, clean shirts, collars and ties and their children in camel's-hair coats, brown velour hats and polished shoes.

And the priest's voice droning on and on to his captive audience.

No, I didn't want any of that. Nor the dancehalls. Stand waiting for the men who had been viewing you like cattle in a market. Their numbers swelling when the public houses closed. Nudging each other. And, when their courage was up, crossing the divide in your direction, you hoped. Though often it was the girl next to you they asked up. I wanted none of it. I'd sign on for another two years.

'You're mad,' said Katy when I announced my decision. 'Everything'll change. Me and Breda gone. All the gorgeous men as well. The camp'll fill up with National Service blokes. Kids just out of school and twerps of Officer Cadets that you can't date anyway. Only ones left will be the regulars. And they're either ancient or married. The girls coming in now are different. You can see that already. Young kids, seventeen and eighteen.'

'But what'll I do if I don't sign on?'

'Go to Glasgow. Steve's there. Get work as a telephonist.'

'Where would I live?'

'Oh, for God's sake! Lots of places. Lodgings. A bedsit. You won't be the only one living alone. There'll be thousands out there.'

I had never had to find a job. I was landed into the one I had. I'd never lived on my own. I'd be afraid. Always I'd shared with other people. You felt safe. Irritated by coughs, by snores. But secure in the presence of others.

Sylvia said, 'Katy, you're forgetting the full-time PT course. She'll have to sign on, otherwise that's off.'

'Why would it be off?' I asked, more startled by the prospect of not achieving my ambition than returning to Ireland.

'Not worth the cost,' Sylvia explained, 'if in six months you'll be gone.'

The next day I signed on for a further two years.

SEVENTEEN

At last I had fulfilled the promise I made to myself in basic training. Hot on the heels of signing on for an extra two years the second course came through. I passed with flying colours. Was promoted to the rank of corporal, had a pay increase of twenty-five shillings a week and was issued with the kit I had hankered after for so long.

As promised, Sylvia bought and stitched on the two stripes and the crossed swords, the insignia of the Physical Training Corps. With Indian ink I whitened them to the brilliance of fresh snow.

I spread the news. Letters to Steve, Bubbles in Santa Barbara, Edith and Marj, care of their home addresses, for we had lost touch. And to my mother I wrote that no longer would she need to feel ridiculed in the post office. I was making her allowance up to ten shillings a week.

In my euphoria I forgot that recently I'd been disappointed with Steve's letters. For no longer did he write page after page of his feelings for me. The letters were shorter and said more about his long hours of study than his longing for me. His small handwriting, once so legible, had become almost impossible to read. Sometimes I gave up trying. Sometimes without looking at his photograph I found it hard to recall his face.

Katy said we should go to the pub and celebrate. We sat on my bed deciding who to invite. I regretted that Connie was already demobilized, positive that this was one party she would have come to. She liked to see women getting on. I'd ask Ginger, some of his regimental police and George. George was my friend. My platonic friend. I had a short explanation—the only bloke who never tried to make me.

'What about Janetta, will you ask her?' Katy asked.

'She'll probably have something on with her bloke.'

'Haven't you noticed she hasn't been about much lately?' Katy replied.

I hadn't. I'd been too wrapped up in my good fortune to notice. I asked Janetta and she said she'd come. And I invited Johnny.

Even though it was my party the men insisted on buying the drinks and crisps. Ginger winked approvingly when he saw me with Johnny, which made me feel guilty. Here I was out with someone I was obviously interested in and poor Steve poring over biology notes or, worse still, a bit of late-night dissecting. Two glasses of cider soon banished any remorse I was feeling as I lost myself in Johnny's lambent, wondrous brown eyes.

We laughed, smoked, drank and sang. George was good-naturedly ragged by the other men. Asked to tell about the cock-up he'd made of his WOSB. Deliberately, according to him. He said the army was a barbaric institution. Barbaric and moronic. 'Shouldn't it have been evident to them that I wasn't officer material? Can you imagine me strutting round with a swagger stick giving orders? I refused to participate in the infantile puzzles and initiative tests.'

'Good on you, George,' someone said. And George puffed with pride. Poor George who always used long words. A fella, they'd say in Ireland, who'd swallowed the dictionary. Even with my scant knowledge of the military mind I couldn't understand why he had been selected to try for a commission. He was the scruffiest soldier I had ever seen. His uniform appeared as if he had slept in it. He wore his beret at an angle no one else did. His boots and webbing never saw blanco or polish. I suppose he was chosen because he had a degree.

He was low-sized and hairy. Shaggy eyebrows, a face that always seemed in need of a shave. When on rare occasions he undid the collar of his tunic, dark hair was visible. He and I had got into talk one morning in the NAFFI. We talked about Dublin. He about visiting the house where Bernard Shaw had been born. And me exclaiming, 'That's only round the corner from where I live. I used to pass it every day. My brother's school was right beside it.' At the time that was the extent of my knowledge of Shaw. It was enough for George. We were friends. Shaw was his hero. In no time I knew the titles of his plays, that he lived in Ayot Saint Lawrence. I was an expert at pretending to listen. I did the same when George tried explaining philosophy. I remember something about a table you can see which in reality you could not. I sucked grass, the sweet juicy stems, or smoked, and George kept talking. I think he liked me. He wrote several times after he finished in the army. Once, with a relation, I went to tea in his bedsit, a small miserable room with dingy curtains and wallpaper, a thin-mattressed bed and a hissing gas fire and ring on which he made pilchards and toast. For pudding we had a Swiss roll of leathery sponge, imitation cream which tasted like ointment and ersatz chocolate. George served the meal with panache. On the floor stacked in piles were volumes of Shaw.

Ginger had laid on a fifteen-hundredweight to take us back to camp after the pub closed. It wasn't far to walk and this Johnny and I chose to do. Arms around each other's waists, stopping now and then to kiss.

'I'm in love,' I told Katy when I was getting ready for bed.

'Again,' she said.

'I can't help it. He's so gorgeous.'

'So is Steve.'

'That's the trouble. I love them both. But it'll sort itself out. Johnny is being posted to the Middle East after Christmas. Then it won't be long until I meet Steve in April. Once I'm engaged I'll never look at another bloke.'

'Janetta's pregnant,' Katy said, lowering her voice.

'Oh God, that's terrible. But still she's engaged so I suppose they'll get married.'

'They won't. He's ditched her. Says he has another girl at home.'

'There's something wrong there. Didn't he take Janetta home to meet his parents?'

'She pretended. They went away for a dirty weekend. He's applied for a posting.'

'Poor Janetta, what'll happen to her?'

'She can't go home. Her family is religious. Which means they go to church and worry about their neighbours.'

'What about the army, what'll they do?'

'She could apply for a discharge under Paragraph Eleven, King's Regulations, and try fending for herself and the kid.'

'Will she?'

'I don't know. She's still in a daze. I could castrate bastards

143

like that. All he had to do was wear a French letter. Selfish sod.'

'She's the only girl I've known since I joined up who got pregnant.'

'There's probably a lot we don't hear of.'

'What d'ye mean?'

'Some who got married and left might have been up the pole. Some might have had abortions. Gone home for a week-end and a handy woman done a job with a crochet hook or knitting needle.'

'You're not serious. Killing a baby! That's a terrible thing. That's a sin.'

'I'd be more worried about bleeding to death or getting sep-tic all through me than sin.'

Janetta went into a home run by the army six weeks before the baby was born, having decided on having the child adopted and coming back into the forces with a posting to another area. The father denied the baby was his and got sent overseas.

There were few maternity clothes for civilians. Those avail-able were grotesque, the waists of skirts enlarged by string or elastic threaded between the buttonhole and fastening to the button. As the belly grew bigger it hitched up the skirts in front. Over this, women wore artist's smocks and loose coats. Janetta had to wear her uniform. Each month she was issued with larger tunics, skirts and greatcoats. Tunics too big in the shoulders, skirts near her ankles. She never went to the NAFFI, ashamed of the stares.

Katy, Sylvia, Breda and I brought her meagre breakfast from the mess. But unless she chose to starve she had to brave the cookhouse at dinner and teatime. I can still see this lovely gentle girl walking into a mess filled with young soldiers whose eyes, even if only for seconds, were drawn to her belly straining against the greatcoat.

* * *

I set out for Brighton with such hopes and expectations that I wore the horrible uniform, thinking that as my family were English they'd be proud to see me in it. And in any case I want-ed to show off my rank.

Waiting at Victoria Station I imagined my reception. How thrilled my aunt would be meeting me for the first time. And how wonderful it would be to meet my grandfather. How he must be looking forward to seeing his dead son's daughter.

At Victoria Station I reread my mother's letter. She was pleased I was going to visit her in-laws. She urged me to write as soon as possible with all the news of what they were like. The way they welcomed me. And not to forget to let my grandfather know that he had a grandson named after him.

I put the letter away and watched the crowds. The majority were uniformed, coming or going on leave, to new postings. And thought how years ago my father and his sister who was nursing in Guys Hospital would have sat here. Maybe on the same seat. I wished it was this sister I was going to meet. She had written to my mother and father from America where she now lived, and when I grew up she sent money, and comics to me, the first tea bags I'd ever seen, and parcels of clothes. She wrote about Paris, how she had lived there as a girl with a sister of her mother's. She encouraged me to learn French and hoped that when the war was over we would meet.

As I sat listening to stations to Brighton being called over the tannoy system, East Croydon, Merstham, Three Bridges, Hayward's Heath, Burgess Hill, I was remembering my father's descriptions of his beloved mother. How small she was. Her long auburn hair. Hair, he said, so long she could sit on it. Her generosity and gaiety. The enormous trays of 'gur cake' she baked to share with children in the street. How she laughed until she cried at shadow pictures on the bedroom walls, thrown there by my father's fingers conjuring images of jumping rabbits, wriggling snakes and the snapping jaws of crocodiles.

Fanny, my high-spirited grandmother who ran away with a Lancer. Whose father never forgave her. Who never allowed her to come home again. Who when introduced to her father-in-law and he asked, 'How are the pigs in Ireland?' replied, 'Ask my sweet Irish arse.'

The aunt I was going to visit looked like her mother. Had the same hair. As the train neared Brighton I wondered if I would recognize her. Would she see a resemblance in me to my father? We'd talk and talk about him. What he was like as a boy. She'd show me the house where they'd lived. Where the night before another sister died her mother had heard 'the three dead knocks' on the wall and knew the child wouldn't live.

And then during the week we'd go to Horsham to see my

grandfather. He'd bring my father alive for me with his reminiscences. He'd have photographs of my grandmother when she was young. Maybe a family picture of the aunts and uncles now scattered all over the world. What a wonderful time I would have.

We'd cry and laugh and talk and talk and talk. I'd be showered with love because I was my father's daughter.

Brighton station. I looked up and down the platform it for a woman with red hair. Slowly I walked along, letting other passengers pass me by. Allowing time for me to be spotted until I was the only person on the platform. No one claimed me.

I waited in the station's entrance. Telling myself my aunt could have been delayed. I waited outside the station still hoping for her arrival. I was cold and hungry. Still I waited. Then took a taxi.

The house was near the racecourse. A three-storey Victorian or Edwardian house. I rang the bell and waited. My spirits had risen again. My heart raced. I was here. In a moment the door would open and I'd be given a hundred thousand welcomes.

The door was opened by a beautiful woman with wavy hair done up in a bun. I said who I was. No exclamations, no hugs, no kisses.

She invited me in. Showed me where to hang my greatcoat and leave my case and then took me into the sitting-room. I was ill at ease. Talked too much. I could see my words hovering above my head like captions in a comic. She asked if I would like some tea. I said, 'That'll be grand. Thanks very much. If you're sure it'll be no trouble. I don't mind waiting. The room is lovely. And that's a lovely fire. It's very cold out.'

I wondered if she was deaf for she only nodded and half smiled. When she left to make the tea I looked around the room. It was big with a bay window where blue velvet hangings were draped. Brass fender and fire irons, the fire's flames reflected in the dazzling brass. Chairs and a long sofa, occasional tables, bookcases, an arrangement of leaves in a vase. Photographs.

She came back with a trolley, tea, sandwiches and rock cakes and she talked. Asked about my mother. She spoke in the same way as officers did. That I found disconcerting, but not as disconcerting as what came next. 'I have a friend,' she said. 'Her son is in the forces and several times he has brought pals home for the weekend. And not one of them has ever offered his mother their ration money.' I immediately offered mine and immediately she took it. I thought of my weekend in Morecambe and Edith's mother.

I asked questions about my grandmother and she replied, 'Actually I remember very little about her. I went away to school when I was eleven and she died shortly afterwards.' And so the time passed awkwardly. Long silences while I racked my brain for something to say. And she replied to questions almost entirely in monosyllables. I was sweating from the strain and the heat of the fire. I asked was it alright if I took off my tunic. 'Do,' she said.

Her husband and daughter came home. They were friendly and welcoming but my aunt never unbent. I began to feel as if I'd come to the wrong house. That I was in a bed and breakfast establishment where the landlady didn't want her guests.

Despite plentiful food and a warm comfortable bedroom I was miserable and felt as if I was a stranger, and decided that the next day I'd complain of feeling unwell and go back to camp. I wondered if my aunt would refund my ration money. Or like a landlady deduct part of it for a cancelled booking. Then I began to console myself. I was a stranger inasmuch as we had never met before. She wasn't Irish. She had spent a long time in her convent school. She was shy. Tomorrow it might be better. And in a couple of days she was taking me to visit my grandfather in Horsham. It would all be different.

It wasn't. Her shyness, reserve or coolness remained the same. And when I met my grandfather I knew who she took after. No kisses or embraces from him either. No mention of my grandmother. Little reference to my father. He asked how my mother was. He asked why I wasn't already married. Most girls of my age were, he said.

He was an elegant old man. Blue-eyed, white-haired, pink-cheeked with a long narrow face, good teeth and an aquiline nose. During the visit he stayed in his chair by the fire, one leg draped gracefully over the other. I didn't care if I never saw him again. I never did. Nor my aunt either.

I was catching a train back to camp at four o'clock. My aunt had an appointment at two o'clock. She made it clear I would leave the house when she did at one-thirty. She put me on a bus for the station, where I had a long wait.

Still smarting, puzzled, and saddened by my reception in Brighton and Horsham, I returned to camp, composing in my mind, as I went, the letter I'd write home. Descriptions of my aunt and grandfather. Their lack of interest in me. How with neither of them did I feel welcome, feel I was their flesh and blood. How seldom my father's name was mentioned. How supposedly religious my aunt was. A daily communicant. With reverently bent head and joined hands walking to the altar to receive. Kneeling longer in her seat, longer than anyone else when she returned. Me glancing sideways at her beautiful thin face with chiselled features like her father's, wings of her glorious hair visible beneath the brown velvet beret. The picture of devotion, of holiness, goodness. Such a hypocrite. Her annoyance when a baby cried at the back of the church. Turning her head to stare coldly at the child's mother. And after mass visiting the crib in adoration before the infant Jesus. The same woman who had let me pay the measly fare to visit my grandfather. On New Year's Eve she announced we would go to the skating rink in Brighton. A treat, I presumed, a making-up to me. Perhaps I had been hasty judging her as miserly. She fed me well. My room was warm and comfortable. She burned good fires. Maybe I was hasty in offering my ration money. Too sensitive. Her mention of it may not have been intended as a hint for me to tip it up. And her cold manner could be shyness. I had never been to an ice rink but assumed that after a few false starts I'd master the technique. I roller-skated regularly in Dublin, I could waltz, do the military two-step. I was good. I would not find skating on ice difficult. But I did. The ice was hard and cold to fall on but the stinging smart wasn't as cold or hurtful as my aunt making it clear, as we approached the ticket office, that I was to buy my own ticket.

I could hear my mother's comments as she read the letter I was composing. 'The hungry cow, the mean bitch, and him, too, to treat a child, an orphan that way. They won't have an hour's luck. But sure what more could you expect from an oul' fella who, before your granny was cold in the clay, sold the family house lock, stock, and barrel. Even your father's school prizes. Never recognize them again.'

* * *

148

The barrack room was deserted. Katy's, Breda's and several other girls' beds were barracked as they would have been left when they went on leave. Unusual. They should have returned before me. Not bothering to make mine up, I dumped my kit bag on the bed and went looking for information. Sylvia would know.

There was a girl I'd never seen before in the clothing store.

'Where's everyone?' I asked.

'Sick, flu, certificates showering in like confetti. I've been posted in to cover. Waiting for my demob … have a fag.' She offered me her packet of Churchman's cigarettes. We chatted for a few more minutes. The extra-strong cigarette made me cough. I nipped it. 'I think I'll wander down to the cookhouse, see if anyone I know is about. Thanks for the fag.'

'Ta, ra for now,' she called after me.

On the way down the slope I met Janetta returning from her daily visit to the cookhouse. Submit to the stares of at least a hundred men or starve. Such a sight she presented. The great-coat tripping her up, the shoulders drooping, the sleeves inches too long. I took her arm and helped her up the slope. Only across her huge belly did the coat fit. She looked sick, tired, dark rings under her eyes, her skin stained with brown pigment. She was panting.

'Not long now,' I said.

'Not long,' she agreed. 'I'm going into the Home in a few weeks.'

'Where is it?'

'Aldershot.'

'We'll visit you, me, Katy and Breda.'

'I'd love that … I won't know anyone in the Home. I finished work last week … but I go down to the exchange every day. Better than sitting in the barrack room on my own. Ginger and the lads are great. I never feel embarrassed with them. Never mention, not even in a joke, my condition … only once Ginge ever made any comment.'

'What did he say?'

'Said if he was my father he'd shoot the bleeder responsible.'

'You've missed your dinner.'

'I'll go to the village later and have something.'

She lay on her bed to get her breath back. I made up mine, talking as I did. I wanted to ask if she'd heard from the bleeder. How she felt about giving her baby up for adoption. But I wasn't sure if she could bear to talk about such things. Instead I gave her an edited version of my stay in Brighton. Conveying that the place wasn't all I had expected. She sat up, struggled out of her greatcoat and threw it over her feet. 'I always thought it was a smashing place. Not a great beach but lots to do. Very popular for "dirty weekends". A lot of hotels and boarding houses … not very fussy.' I wondered if it was to Brighton her bloke took her when she'd told us it was to meet his parents. I noticed she no longer wore her engagement ring.

'Have you seen Johnny about?'

Janetta said she had not, and by the time I'd finished making my bed she was snoring softly. There were two letters from Steve. Almost impossible to read but with a lot of concentration I deciphered the scribbles … 'Sometimes I regret doing medicine. Between lectures, taking notes, and studying … never mind dissecting … there's little time left. But it's supposed to improve when you go to the wards.'

Briefly he mentioned missing me and looking forward to our meeting in Crewe and becoming engaged. This set me wondering where we would stay. Would he expect me to sleep with him once I was manacled by a ring? I couldn't. I wouldn't. A ring guaranteed nothing. Janetta had had a ring. I went looking for Johnny. Stopping at the married quarters of my friends, I suddenly realized how hungry I was. I'd eaten nothing since my breakfast in Brighton. Betty would give me a piece of her delicious lemon meringue pie or some of her crunchy flapjacks and Nescafé. I adored Nescafé.

There was no one in. I felt cold and shivery, the way I often felt at home. A feeling I'd never experienced since I came to this camp. A presentiment that I was going to hear bad news. I set off for the village, telling myself it was the cold. A wind had risen and I was hungry. I ran down the slope. The running warmed me and the smell of hot food cheered me a little. The jukebox was playing and the pinball machines ringing and clanging and tables with men I knew sitting round them. But of Johnny no sign.

'Over here, Pad,' a soldier called, indicating an empty chair. Someone else bought me coffee and an Eccles cake. The men talked. Johnny was on a detail. Wouldn't be back until after dinner. Rumours were floating round. Unit being suspended. Short Service commissions in Aldershot now. Regulars in Sandhurst,

Royal Mechanical and Electrical Engineers taking over here. No one knew for sure. Could be just another bloody rumour. In any case who cared? Their demob was coming up.

Was it a presentiment of a move that was depressing me? Everyone I knew and loved would be scattered and God alone knew where I might finish up. And nowhere could compare with here. This magical place where all I'd known was happiness. My land of joy, of eternal youth, my Tír na nÓg. I left a message with one of Johnny's mates. I would meet him in the NAFFI at seven o'clock.

* * *

His eyes were like black velvet, his teeth dazzling in his wide smile. I wanted to eat him. I wanted to be in his arms, my head on his breast. I wanted to smell his gorgeous smell.

While we ate our supper I told him about my trip to Sussex. He was appalled. He came from a big, close, extended family. He couldn't imagine any of his mother's people treating him as I had been treated. They were from Liverpool. His father from South Africa. The relations kept in touch and, now that the war was over, planned to visit each other. I ranted and raved throughout the meal about my aunt and grandfather. Now and then he reminded me to eat, not to let the chips go cold. And while we drank our coffee he said, 'You won't visit them again in a hurry.'

'Never, ever,' I replied, looking at his handsome face, wanting to leave the canteen and be in his arms.

'I think,' he said, reading my thoughts, 'there'll be little shelter from the wind even in the deepest porch tonight. How about the cricket pavilion?'

'Are you mad, we'd freeze to death on the steps of the pavilion.'

'Who said anything about the steps. Look at what I've got.' And before my eyes he waved a bunch of keys. 'I know the groundsman, I swapped my cigarette ration for these.' He jingled the keys.

'You mean we can go inside?'

'Go inside. Make tea. Have a shower. Whatever you fancy except smoke.'

'Why no smoking?'

'The pavilion is ancient. There since the last war. Dry as tinder. One spark and whoosh.'

We were careful to make sure no one saw us approach the building. Taking a last look round we mounted the few steps.

'I brought a torch,' Johnny whispered, inserting the key into the lock.

Once the door was opened a mixture of smells wafted out. Leather and wood, liniment. Maybe I imagined the smell of crushed grass. I was never interested in cricket but found the ambience at a match delightful. The snowy-clad figures against the green field, the sound of leather on wood and what appeared to me a leisurely, gentle sport.

Shielding the torch with his hand, Johnny checked that the windows were shuttered before taking off our greatcoats and laying them of the floor where we sat on them. We kissed and stroked each other's faces. Told how much we loved and missed each other. My heart raced with the nearness of him and guilty excitement knowing we were in a forbidden place. We lay down. He undid my tunic and moved his hands over my breasts. I played with his ear lobe, a technique someone told me men liked. His kissing became more passionate. It was a time when somewhere else we would have smoked. He would have extricated himself from my embrace, lit two cigarettes, and placed one between my lips. He moved away from me and asked, 'What about Steve?'

'What about him?'

'Will you get engaged? D'ye love him?'

'I did when he left. Then I met you. Now I'm not so sure.'

'And the meeting in Crewe. Will you go?'

'I'll have to. He's coming down from Glasgow in the middle of the night.'

'He's a nice bloke. Nice-looking too. Fair hair and blue eyes. Same as that kid, Mary, you're so crazy about.'

'I suppose he is a bit.'

'I bet if you had a baby that's the sort you'd like, fair and blue-eyed.'

'You have to take what God sends.'

I was uneasy at the way the conversation was going without knowing why. Kissing was the way to stop it. Put Steve out of his mind. So I tried a passionate kiss but he put me away from him and spoke again.

'Maybe you won't have to decide between us.'

'What d'ye mean?'

I dreaded his answer. He was going to pack me in. Say we were cheating. Being unfair to Steve. Unfair to him. I must love Steve, otherwise why go to Crewe?

'There's a chance I may be posted to the Middle East.'

'Oh God, I'll die if you are.'

'No you won't. You'll find someone else, or maybe grow up and settle for Steve.'

'I don't want someone else. It's you I love.'

He traced the outline of my lips and said, 'And I love you. I've never loved a girl before. I'll always love you. I want to marry you but it's not that simple.'

'But it is. I'll write to Steve. Tell him the truth. It'll be fine. No problem.'

I wanted to marry Johnny. Be married, there and then. Lie in my skin next to him. Let him do all the things my body ached for. Be his wife. Not afraid of pregnancy. Not afraid of losing his respect.

'Ah,' he said, 'there's more to it than Steve. It's something we'd have to do a lot of talking about; a lot of thinking about.'

'Talk now. Tell me now.' I was frightened and impatient.

'I'm afraid to. It's not easy.'

'Afraid?' I was angry. I stood up. 'Afraid, what do you mean afraid?'

'To talk to you about it. I wish we could smoke. And keep your voice down.'

'You're married, that's it, isn't it. Don't lie. Katy can find out from the office.' I was crying. 'All the time you've been a married man.'

'No. No. I'm not married. It's something else. I can't explain it now. But I love you. I always will. Remember that. We'd better make a move.'

He dried my face and helped me on with my greatcoat and we left the hut as cautiously as we had entered.

'I'll see you tomorrow,' he bent down to kiss me. I pulled away and said, 'No, not tomorrow. I don't want to see you until you tell me.' And I rushed into the billet.

I avoided going to the NAFFI at times he might be there and didn't go to the café. I went to my friend in the married quarters and sobbed out my story. She fed me, trimmed my hair and tried to cheer me up. She told me how she had gone out to South Africa to marry Sean, her husband. In cases where the couple intended could prove the seriousness of their intent, the army paid for a passage out. Sean was stationed in Cape Town, seconded there instructing South Africans in the use of modern artillery weapons.

'I hadn't seen him for a year,' she said. 'I was beginning to forget what he looked like.'

I knew the feeling, having sometimes experienced difficulty in recalling Steve's face.

'I met a white South African on the boat. He was very attractive. When I told him I was going to Cape Town to marry he became concerned. Asked me lots of questions. Where was Sean from? Did I know his people? I told him I did. He was a Kerryman. A soldier. I asked him why he was so concerned. He said that he wondered if I had seen this chap, that he could have been coloured. Thinking of Sean's blue eyes, such a typically Irish face, I laughed as I described it to him. That's all right then, he said, but told me if I had seen only a photograph it could be deceptive. That not all Cape coloured were coal-black niggers. That there were many variations because of intermarrying and interbreeding over hundreds of years. In some cases only a very discerning eye could spot it.'

She changed the subject and talked about the weather. How very cold it was. She made tea and Spam sandwiches and while we were eating and drinking casually said, 'Johnny's very dark-skinned, isn't he?'

'Olivey, I sometimes wonder if he's Jewish.'

'I wouldn't think so. A different slant to his features. Lovely looking. And his teeth. The only other place I've seen teeth like that was in South Africa.'

'His father's from there. He's hoping to go on a visit now the war's over.'

Again she changed the subject, telling me about the little boy she had buried before coming to the camp.

'Meningitis. Tubercular. He was five years old. The image of Sean. He died in Tidworth Hospital. He was in a ward with American soldiers. They used to have bananas flown in for him. He was a long time dying. Now they have a drug, a miracle drug that might have saved him. Streptomycin. I read about it the other day ... Don't cry, hinny. He's in Heaven.'

She was a convert with a strong faith.

'Does Mary look like him?'

'A bit. The same blonde hair and blue eyes.'

'Johnny said last night that if I had a baby I'd want one that looked like Mary. He loves her but I think he's a bit jealous. He says I'm crazy about her. I am. All the same I thought it was a queer thing for him to say.'

We toasted ourselves before the fire. Mary was having her afternoon nap and Sean was in work, so we talked for ages. She told me about the Depression. The terrible poverty in Newcastle where she came from, and where her father had a butcher's shop. Some of his customers were miners' wives who'd come in for four penn'orth of bones and how he'd always include some scraps of meat. How her mother threatened he'd bankrupt himself. How her uncle, who was the bailiff for the local duke, brought meat from her father's shop to the estate. Sides of beef, whole lambs, and veal carcasses.

'Sometimes he'd take me for the ride. The cook made a great fuss of me. She had a thing about my uncle but he was happily married. Such a huge kitchen it was and full of food. Earthenware bowls full of eggs, baskets of freshly picked mushrooms. Cakes and loaves of bread cooling. One of the maids would take me into the dairy where I could help myself to cream. As much as I could eat. Thick, thick cream. Basins and basins of it. So much of everything. All the meat my uncle had brought, and in the cold room hares, rabbits, all sorts of game hanging ... Have a cup of Nescafé?'

I never refused anything she offered me. She brought in the tray with the coffee, laid it on the table and threw a shovelful of coal on the fire. Then she settled herself, her beautiful voluptuous body, in an armchair, lit a cigarette and said, 'I was just wondering if maybe Johnny is coloured. If that's what he's afraid of telling you.'

'But he's not black. He's not a nigger. I've seen niggers on the pictures. He doesn't look like them.'

'They don't all look the same. Each tribe looks different. Some are very beautiful. I wasn't thinking about a full-blown black man. He could have a lick of the tarbrush.'

'What's that?'

'One of his parents, grandparents, even further back, could have been a native. It was asking about blonde, blue-eyed babies that made me think. Though I did occasionally wonder the time you

155

brought him here. He reminded me of men I'd seen in Cape Town.'

'But that's no reason to be afraid. I wouldn't care if he was.'

'You might have a black baby.'

'How could that happen? He's not black.'

'It can. You've heard people say a child is the image of his granny or grandfather … they can be the same colour as well.'

'I still wouldn't care.'

'He might for your sake. Coloured people don't have an easy time of it. And there's your mother. What would she say?'

'I suppose if he turned Catholic she wouldn't mind. In any case we would stay in England. No one at home would have to know. But I don't believe it. He isn't coloured.'

Mary woke, liverish as she always was after her sleep, ignoring me. Wanting only her mother. As I got up to leave, Betty said, 'Think about what I told you. And if you make it up in the heat of the moment don't get carried away.'

She was forever drumming this advice into Katy, Breda and me, adding in her lovely Geordie accent that an unwanted baby was too high a price to pay.

I kept away from the NAFFI and the café, but hoped when going about the camp or to and from the exchange, I'd bump into Johnny. I chatted with the telephonist on duty in between her calls. We wondered when the girls away sick would be back. She moaned about the longer shifts she was now working. Then laughed, 'Four hours instead of two and I'm complaining. It'll be a hell of a lot different in Civvy Street, I bet, there's not many two-hourly shift jobs out there.'

I told her how I'd fallen out with Johnny, how I'd stormed off and regretted it, but that I wouldn't be the first one to give in.

'I think he's smashing-looking. Are you serious about him?'

'I don't know. The trouble with me is I don't know what I want. One minute I want to be married and the next just go on enjoying myself. Falling in love with someone new. That's the best part. Fancying a bloke. Wanting him to ask you out but once he does it's never the same. The thrill goes out of it. Well, with some blokes it does.'

'Would you marry Johnny?'

'When he gets me all worked up I want to be married. D'ye really think he's smashing-looking?'

'Gorgeous, very Italian-looking.'

'Now that you come to mention it, he is. I never thought of that. I suppose because his name's not Italian.'

'Could be on his mother's side. Are you missing the PT lessons?'

'A bit. Not much else to do. I expect they'll be back soon, then I'll be moaning about having too much work.'

Walking back to the billet I wondered why it hadn't occurred to me that Johnny was Italian. I told myself it was because before Betty put ideas into my head I didn't care what he was.

* * *

Except for Janetta's soft snoring the barrack room was quiet, lonely. I decided to go for my tea. Ask an orderly to make a few sandwiches for Janetta. I'd be glad when she was gone. In the Home she'd be saved the trudge to the cookhouse, the embarrassment of appearing in her greatcoat before the soldiers.

When I came back it was bedlam. A group of girls newly posted in. A couple of them by Janetta's bed. Another one setting up a portable radio, tuning it in. Radio Luxembourg blaring out songs I wasn't familiar with. Cocky, confident girls already at home. Kids; eighteen, seventeen. Calling me Corp. I wanted to reprimand them. Say, 'When you speak to me, my rank is Corporal.' Only I didn't have the nerve and couldn't be that pompous. But their music and shrieks of laughter were giving me a headache. Five minutes in the place and already they were taking over. Our place. Then I caught myself on. I was jealous of their high spirits. Of their possessions. I was getting old, cranky. Resenting newcomers. It wasn't my place. But as an NCO it was my place to make them welcome, show them the ropes. I calmed down. Spoke to them. Told them where to go for their tea.

One who had been talking to Janetta said, 'Poor cow, he's a sod. We'll give the cookhouse a miss. Janetta told us there's a caff, we'll try that and bring her back chips. Keep the radio on if you want. This is how you turn it off or down,' she demonstrated. I decided they were OK and listened to the music and songs. 'Ballin' the Jack', I liked that. So did Janetta, who made me laugh as she attempted to dance to it.

EIGHTEEN

Katy, Breda and Sylvia came back from sick leave. I told them about falling out with Johnny. About Betty's suggestion that he might be coloured and that if I married him I could have a coloured baby.

Katy and Sylvia thought it was possible. Breda who, like me, had seldom seen a coloured man except on the pictures, dismissed the idea.

'He doesn't look a bit like one. Remember the one in 'Gone with the Wind'?'

But Katy and Sylvia, coming from more cosmopolitan cities, said coloured people came in all shapes and sizes. Katy didn't think it mattered if he was. What counted was whether I loved him or not. She didn't think I did.

'No more than you love Steve. With you it's the idea of being in love. If Johnny left tomorrow you'd lose no sleep over him. Remember how quickly you recovered after Steve went?'

I turned on her and shrewishly said, 'You're in no position to talk. You flit from one bloke to another like a bee gathering honey.'

'True,' she said, 'but I don't kid myself I've fallen for them.'

'Maybe it's just that you never fall in love.'

'I did once,' she said, and I remembered her story of the Canadian sweetheart who hadn't returned from the Dieppe raid. Sylvia, not to be left out of the conversation, brought it around to her engagement to Hutch, reminding us that he had been coloured. And how because of it she had broken it off.

'We know,' snapped Katy, 'you've told it all before. Mammy and Daddy wouldn't have approved. Though according to another version of your story, they'd already been dead for years.'

Breda, the peacemaker, intervened. 'Come on you lot, you're all being very ratty tonight.'

We were and realized it. Blamed it on the after-effects of the flu, long train journeys and hunger.

'We'll all go to the NAFFI for a scoff,' said Sylvia. 'My treat.'

Johnny might be there. I was longing to see him. To make it up. Forget about South Africans and black babies. I wouldn't nag for an explanation of his fear. That would come in time. Tonight I wanted his presence. His arms. His kisses.

'Eh, it's parky,' Sylvia said as we went outside. We turned up the collars of our greatcoats and walked briskly to the canteen, commenting on the sudden change in the weather.

The NAFFI was hot, steamy and smoky and as always reeking of fat. I had a good look round but Johnny was not there.

A girl who worked in Katy's office came in and joined us. She was crying and asking, 'Have you heard the news yet? Oh my God I can't believe it. You know Dora, my mate? Well, she's dead …'

'But I saw her only …' Sylvia began to say.

'Before she went on leave. I know, we all did, I travelled as far as London with her. She was from up north. I left her going to King's Cross.'

'How do you know? Who told you?' asked Katy.

'Word came through this afternoon. It'll be on Orders tomorrow. Meningitis. Three days sick, that's all.'

We found it hard to believe. She was our age. Strong and healthy. Very smart. Slim. Fuzzy, short fair hair. She swung an accent and was a snob. Not very popular. Now everyone remembered only her good points. We shed tears. I was still crying while I was undressing for bed. Katy said I was too soft-hearted and Breda advised a few prayers for her soul. They'd have given other advice could they have seen into my mind and the thoughts going through it. I was crying for myself. Crying with terror that Death could strike so suddenly. That I hadn't left it behind in Ireland …

I woke next morning feeling desperately sick. I had a blinding headache, a stiff neck, my hand on my forehead registered a temperature and the light streaming in through the curtainless windows hurt my eyes. Meningitis. I recognized the symptoms. I shouted for Breda, clutched her arm and implored her to get the doctor, the medical orderly.

'I'm so sick. I think I'm dying. Get someone quick. Tell them I'm too ill to go on sick parade.'

She went for Sylvia, and Katy came to my aid. Held my head and a glass of water to my lips.

'You look OK to me. Drink this. Maybe you're getting the flu.'

Flu-like symptoms was often how meningitis began. I moaned. Sylvia arrived and was very sympathetic. 'You stay in bed, chuck. I'll nip over to the Medical Inspection Room. If there's no one there yet I'll tell Miss Long. She used to be a nurse be-fore joining up. And I'll fetch you a cup of tea.'

Breda brought a cold flannel for my forehead. It wasn't properly wrung out and drips ran down my face. Katy left me a packet of fags and matches. Poor Janetta, waddling round like a duck, was very solicitous and assured the others she would look after me until help arrived.

Which it did in the person of Miss Long. Dying as I sup-posed myself to be, her brisk movements, wiry silver hair curling round her cap and alert, brown eyes again reminded me of a fox terrier.

'You're too ill to report sick, so I'm told,' she said, coming to my bed, laying a freezing-cold hand on my forehead. 'So what ails you?'

She shook down the thermometer.

'My head has a terrible pain. My neck is stiff and the light hurts my eyes,' I replied in a faint voice.

She took my temperature and felt my pulse.

'Your temperature is normal. Sit up and open your pyjama jacket.'

She scrutinized my chest, belly and back. And announced in her brisk no-nonsense voice, 'You're hysterical or malingering.'

'I am not, ma'am. I've got meningitis.' I began to cry.

'You've no such thing. Private Pearson contracted her dis-ease miles from here. You've a head cold, a crick in your neck and your eyes are affected by the glare of the sun shining on the snow. It snowed heavily during the night. Get up, shower and dress. Call into my office. I'll give you a chit for late breakfast. A walk in the fresh air will clear your head.'

She left the room.

Janetta said I looked better and offered to come with me to the cookhouse. Poor, kind Janetta willing to risk the slope.

'No,' I thanked her. Said I'd pick up the chit but not use it. 'I'll have a char and wad in the NAFFI.' I'd be there in time for break. See the girls and hopefully Johnny.

The day was glorious. Sunshine and a brilliant blue sky. The landscape had been transformed. Bare branches layered with snow, thick as frosting on a Christmas cake. Icicles hanging from the eaves of buildings reflecting prisms of colour. The snow criss-crossed with imprints of birds' feet. Fluffed-out robins displaying their breasts.

I was invigorated. Breathed in lungfuls of the crisp, cold air. I momentarily forgot meningitis, Dora and my loss of Tír na nÓg. My cheeks glowed. And I felt glad to be alive as I crunched my way to the canteen.

Johnny wasn't there. Choosing to forget that it was I who had sent him packing, I decided he was deliberately avoiding me. And that I never wanted to see him again, though every time the door opened I looked to see if it was him.

The girls were there. We sat drinking tea and talking. Breda suggested we should have a Mass said for Dora and send the card to her parents. Sylvia wasn't in favour. 'Don't forget she wasn't a Catholic. It might offend,' adding, 'We could send a sympathy letter.' We agreed that was a good idea. Sylvia volunteered to write it. In a couple of days we forgot our good intentions and the letter was never written.

It was Wednesday, our afternoon off for recreation, and as all sports fixtures were cancelled because of the weather we were free to spend it as we chose. We would make a giant snowman. Soldiers we knew agreed to help. Sylvia, who was pally with a cook, borrowed a huge tray to use as a toboggan. So after dinner we gathered on the cricket field and played with the delight and exuberance of children on the first day of snow. With his khaki cap the snowman had a military air. He sported a twig pipe and pebbles we'd scrambled for as his buttons. To complete his soldierly bearing someone found a stick to tuck under his arm as if it was a swagger cane.

A snowball fight was organized—girls versus men. We screamed and giggled as the men chased and caught us. Pretended indignation as they rubbed snow into our faces and down our necks. Titillated and excited as their fingers lingered. Our fingers and toes ached with cold. We stamped our feet and blew on our fingers. Made a gigantic snowball and sent it hurling down a steep slope. Took turns tobogganing down less steep ones. Screamed and laughed with delight, and hoped a thaw wouldn't set in for a few days.

I was desperate for contact with Johnny and hoped and prayed that on the way down to tea my wish would be granted. It was. He was riding in the back of a truck. God, he was so beautiful. Katy was wrong. I really and truly loved him. I adored him. But at the same time I felt resentful. He was being secretive. Why couldn't he confide in me? He had to be married. He had strung me along. And in the instant it took me to reach this conclusion I ignored his wave and whistle. The truck drove on.

The next morning there was an ominous silence in the atmosphere. The sky was leaden and there was not a glimpse of the sun. And so began the winter of 1947. One of the coldest since records began. My spirits sank. I went for a bath and noticed purple bruising on my inner thighs. Fear squeezed my heart. Another symptom of meningitis. I knew it. I wasn't hysterical or a malingerer. I felt faint, shivering and sweating. I'd got the dreadful disease. Then I remembered tobogganing—the tray biting and banging into my thighs—and made a miraculous recovery.

PT lessons were cancelled. Clerks, orderlies and telephonists reported for work as usual. From the window I watched snow falling, each flake unique and exquisitely shaped. Some coming to rest on window panes, melting, their tears trickling down the glass.

One freezing day followed another. Our warm barracks room became chilly as power to the radiators was reduced to economize on fuel. Little by little the heating was diminished. Little by little the hot water cooled. Fuel supplies were unable to get through. Most of the country was affected.

Only the hardiest bathed or showered. The rest made do with topping and tailing. Knickers froze on radiators. Daily changing of underwear became a thing of the past.

And snow still fell and the wind howled. It blew the snow into drifts against the spider's door. Our world had changed, I thought, forever. Never again would there be sun, never again skies that weren't leaden.

Our plethora of kit contained every item of clothing except wellington boots or galoshes, so that after walking a short distance feet were soaked. I ventured only as far as Betty's and the telephone exchange or tidied again and again my storeroom. It had once been a men's urinal; the basins were still against the walls, the waterscale or urine stains embedded in the porcelain, the stink lingering after all the years. Fully dressed, capped and gloved I made lists of skipping ropes, bean bags, quoits, net-balls, until numb fingers stopped me from writing.

In Betty's I warmed in front of the Primus, for which she still had plenty of paraffin, and drank Nescafé. In the Exchange I drank sergeant-major's tea—lukewarm, having cooled in the few minutes it took to bring it from the cookhouse. The coke-burning stove was kept going on anything that would burn. A meagre ration of coke supplemented with twists of paper, maga-zines, tatty books, scrapings from the dinner plates. I'd put my shoes on top of the stove where they dried like biltong. They crippled my feet when I had to put them on again.

* * *

Johnny seemed to have vanished off the face of the earth. Steve's letters took longer to arrive. I felt forlorn and unloved. I stopped going to the café. Not to avoid Johnny but to escape trudging through the snow, slipping and sliding on the icy road and the biting wind that found its way through all my layers of clothing. And so I didn't fall in love with anyone for the time being.

* * *

Eventually the radiators' minute output of heat was turned off. Our beds, the only place where there had been a degree of com-fort, no longer had that to offer. Without the central heating they became damp and the sheets and pillowcases had an icy chill to them. We stripped them off and spread them on top of the blankets. Removed only caps, shoes, tunics and skirts and used the clothing, greatcoats, civilian clothes, extra towels, any-thing that would spread on the bed, to trap whatever heat our bodies generated in shivering fits. Betty filled hot-water bottles for us. We carried them back to the barrack room tucked inside our greatcoats, but by the time we arrived they were lukewarm. Every day we consoled ourselves and each other that this weather couldn't last much longer. It did. We soldiered on with chilblains, chapped hands and lips. But there was worse to come. Field kitchens were set up when the fuel supply ran out. Shallow trenches were dug into the ground into which burners resembling enormous blow lamps were placed. Metal plates lined the trenches and supported huge containers filled with food, which was cooked by the fierce heat from the burners. The field kitchen was set up outside the cookhouse. And in the Arctic conditions we queued for our meals. The main meal was always stew. Stew of some indescribable meat which floated in a fatty, greasy liquid to which root vegetables were later added. Shivering and miserable, we carried plates of the revolting food into the cookhouse to eat. Our previous meals, often described as pig swill, were now recalled as gourmet dishes. I seem to remember vast quantities of beetroot being served. Tinned, vinegary beetroot. We were ravenous and ate whatever was served, mopping our plates with chunks of bread.

Janetta was finally excused from going to the cookhouse. The revolting messes were delivered to the barrack room and she was forbidden from going outside. She did one day, fell and went into labour. Despite the gritting of the roads, the journey to the hospital was slow, getting her there only in the nick of time to deliver her baby girl. Aldershot was miles away, buses not running, and no lifts to be had … Breda, ever the optimist, was sure that once Janetta was settled somewhere, she would contact us. Katy, being realistic, said she wouldn't. 'She'll want to put this place out of her mind. Make a fresh start.' Katy was right. We never heard from her.

It seemed as if we were condemned to live in misery forever. Lousy food, freezing beds, chapped hands and lips. Chilblains that throbbed and itched. No love. No letters. And then we woke one morning and the sun was shining. We weren't condemned to live forever beneath a leaden sky. We laughed, sang, danced and asked the new girls to turn up the radio. We were reborn. The thaw set in. Snow fell from roofs with a great swooshing sound. Birds that had survived rooted in the ground. And, being on high ground, we were spared the misery of flooding.

The fuel supply was restored, radiators switched on, the water ran hot and the field kitchen was dismantled. Physical training was reinstated. After a very short time it was difficult to remember that so recently we had shivered and experienced such discomfort.

I rejoiced with everyone else, but knew a change had taken place in me which had started in Brighton. Being rejected by those I had presumed would show me affection, then Dora dying, Betty's talk about coloured people, my quarrel with Johnny, Janetta's misfortune—so many unpleasant happenings in a short time. Never again would I be so completely carefree, never again believe that this camp was a place of permanent happiness. I had grown up.

NINETEEN

During the next week I saw Johnny several times. Sometimes in the distance. Several times close by. Each of us waiting for the other to make the first move. I yearned for him to say something, to reach out, touch me. Longed for courage to take the initiative. Neither of us acknowledged the other.

'You sent him packing. It was up to you to do something,' Katy said when I related what was happening. 'Write a note—he'll come flying.'

But anger, pride or fear that he might not come flying stopped me. I consoled myself that there was plenty of time. That eventually I'd get round to writing. But plenty of time there wasn't. At short notice I had to attend a games course in Aldershot. And when I came back after two weeks away Johnny had left camp. Gone on embarkation leave.

He would be at home for ten days and after that in the depot at Woolwich, where he would join a batch of artillery men due to travel to Egypt in April.

All this he wrote in a letter awaiting me. Reading the date on which it was written I saw that he would already be at the regimental depot. Also in his letter he repeated what he had told me many times, how he loved me and always would. That once he was settled in his new posting he would write and tell what it was he feared.

'While I was with you I couldn't pluck up courage, afraid you might throw me over. You did anyway. You'll never know how that shocked me. Not at first because I thought it was just a tiff that would blow over in no time. But after you ignored me in the lorry I knew it was serious. Like a fool I then went out of my way to avoid you. So a letter is now the only way left. You'll then have time to think about the problem. Talk it over with your mother, friends, your padre, and make up your mind. Maybe since we split you have finally decided that Steve is the one you want to marry. I hope not but I'll understand and won't love you any the less. Always remember that. And the good times we had.

Loving you forever,
Johnny.'

He enclosed in his letter the British Forces overseas address and a photograph of himself. His wonderful eyes looked at me—pleading, I imagined. I kissed the picture and stroked his olive-coloured skin while tears streamed down my face.

I had to do something positive, I realized. Find out if he was married. That was easy. Katy looked up his records. He was single, British and Church of England. One by one my worries fell away. If he was English he couldn't be coloured. Religion wasn't a problem. My grandfather was a Protestant. I wasn't religious. Nowadays I often missed mass, seldom went to confession. And my mother, not that I'd let her stand in my way, wouldn't object. Not if we married in England. The neighbours wouldn't know it was a mixed marriage. But after a few more tears and a few more cigarettes I came down to earth. Asking myself what was it he was afraid of if all the things I had found out were OK. My fertile imagination ran riot. Perhaps he had murdered someone. Perhaps he'd done time in prison. Would that be on his army documents? And the thought which made me cry again, that he had some dreadful disease. One the army hadn't discovered. One that ran in his family. That wouldn't show itself for years.

'My poor, poor love,' I said to his picture. 'Did you think that I'd mind that? I'd nurse you. Look after you for the rest of your life. Why didn't you trust me? We could have been married by now.'

I was going to see him. Going to Woolwich. See him before he sailed. Maybe we could get a special license. I'd apply for a forty-eight-hour pass. Woolwich wasn't far away. Convince him that whatever he feared I didn't. I would give Steve up. We'd get married before he sailed.

I wouldn't tell Katy or Breda my plans. Breda'd be genuinely upset at the idea of me marrying an unbeliever, someone who'd never get to heaven. Katy'd tell me that I was mad. That I didn't love him. Didn't trust him. That if I went ahead and married him he'd still be sent to Egypt. He wouldn't get a married quarter in a hurry. Wasn't senior enough, married long enough, or in the army long enough to have many points. By the time we moved up the list he'd be back in England where I'd have spent two lonely years. Lonely or flirting about from one bloke to another. And having lost any excuse for prizing my virginity, I'd have already lost it. Once gone it was gone forever. You knew what it was all about. If you'd enjoyed the experience you'd want a repeat performance.

There I knew she was wrong. I'd be a faithful wife. Never look at another man. After all, I was a Catholic and adultery was a mortal sin.

Sylvia would be more understanding and would lend me money for the trip. Then, remembering that I wasn't confiding in Katy and Breda and that Sylvia wasn't the best at keeping secrets, I decided to go see Betty instead. She'd lend the money. Sean was there, having finished work early. I was invited to stay for tea. Pilchards in tomato sauce, a meal I hated. But with rationing still in force, you ate what you got. I loved Betty and Sean for their warmth, generosity, and humour. Only recently had I realized that it wasn't just for these qualities and his extraordinary good looks that I felt about Sean as I did. He was the age my father would have been had he lived. He was my father figure. And often acted as one. Concerned about my future, reminding me how important it was for a girl to get a good job. I would laugh at him when he suggested that it should carry a pension. And he'd respond, 'You may well laugh, but I'm serious. Who's to say, you may choose not to marry.'

He was from Kerry, where there's a long tradition of matchmaking. He thought there was much to be said for it, though he admitted his match to Betty had been the result of him picking her up in a truck as she waited for a bus.

After tea I told them the purpose of my visit.

'If course I'll let you have the money,' said Betty, 'but I'm not sure going to Woolwich is a good idea, are you Sean?'

'Let me tell you about Woolwich. There are hundreds of men there. Waiting to go overseas, waiting for demob. They parade in the morning and book in at night. In the meantime, they disperse all over the city. Most doing part-time work. Lyons Corner Houses are great favourites. Dishwashing. Then the pubs, then back to barracks. No one knows who is who. Unless you write to him before going up, it'd be like looking for a needle in a haystack.'

'I was planning on going tomorrow.'

'Take my advice and don't.'

I had brought the photograph of Johnny with me and showed it to them. Though they had met him on numerous occasions Sean now looked intently at the picture. Handing it back, he said, 'What Johnny's afraid to tell you is that he's coloured.'

'But he's not. You've seen him. We've babysat for you dozens of times. He's not a black man.'

'How many coloured people have you seen?'

'A few. Students from Trinity on my last leave. They were jet black. Like the ones in American pictures. How can you be so sure about Johnny?'

'I was in South Africa for years. I always knew Johnny was coloured. It didn't seem important. He was just one of your here-today-gone-tomorrow boyfriends. He's a nice bloke. But not for you to marry.'

'But I want to marry him.'

'You'll live to regret it. Both of you.'

'Why would we regret it if we love each other?'

'It's always better to marry your own kind. Marriage isn't just about love. God knows there's little enough tolerance of different religions and nationalities, but less when colour is involved. If you marry him you're in for a hard time. You won't, once he's out of the army, find it easy getting a place to live. Work won't be easy to come by. And think about the children you may have.'

I knew he meant well. I didn't resent his advice but had no intention of taking it. But because I was so fond of him and Betty I decided to pretend I would.

'I expect you're right and going to Woolwich probably isn't such a good idea. So thanks all the same, Betty, I won't need the money now,' I lied. I'd borrow from Sylvia and risk her telling Katy and Breda.

'That's sensible. Write to Johnny, no harm in that. He'll be gone for two years. Let time take care of things. And after all you may come back from Crewe flashing your diamonds,' Betty said, smiling tolerantly. And Sean added, 'I know the very man for you. Posted in yesterday. Tall, good-looking, a Catholic and a sergeant who'll go far. You'll see him around. But in any case, I'll invite you to the mess next Saturday and introduce you.'

They smiled at me affectionately and Betty promised to do my hair before we went to the mess.

* * *

Sylvia lent me the money and promised not to tell Katy and Breda. 'But they'll wonder where you've gone,' she warned.

I said I'd think of something before putting in for my pass.

As it turned out I never got to Woolwich. I woke the next morning with an itch. Looked at my hands, in between my fingers, and knew what ailed me. Scabies. I'd had them during the war when they were endemic in Dublin. In the bathroom I examined myself and in my groin and armpits were the minute red spots where the mites were burrowing under my skin and laying their eggs. I knew the cure. Scalding baths in which rock sulphur had been dissolved. But where in the village would I get rock sulphur? And if I could, its rotten-egg smell would cause a riot. I'd have to report sick. Untreated scabies caused constant itching and became infected. It was several years since I'd had them. There was probably a more up-to-date treatment.

There was. It involved hospital isolation. By lunchtime I was on the train to the skin hospital in Hindhead. Soon after arrival I stood naked in a cubicle where a pretty older woman orderly sympathized with my condition. And then with a shaving brush lathered me with a thick white substance from neck to feet, front and back. Long lingering brush-strokes. Particularly long and lingering in the belly and breast area. And all the while complimenting me on my figure. I felt ill at ease without knowing why. While I was dressing she called through the cubicle curtains, 'Bath in the morning then report here at ten o'clock.'

'How long does the treatment last?' I called back.

'Three to five days, three usually.'

Mine took five. After two more days of lavishing strokes and compliments the orderly changed her manner to one of briskness. Only years later did it occur to me that she may have been making a pass at me.

I enjoyed the five days of leisure. After morning inspection, when patients stood by their beds while the senior medical officer, matron and nurses did the ward round, I was free to do what I wished. I read, and wrote letters to Johnny at his home address, Woolwich and the British Forces overseas.

Letters full of love and longing. Letters saying how eagerly I was waiting to hear from him and discover what it was he had feared telling me. How there was nothing in the world so terrible that could alter my love for him. I told him that the nearer my meeting with Steve came the more convinced I was that it would be the end of our affair. I might not go to Crewe. Since I was certain that I no longer loved him it seemed pointless. But on the other hand he deserved to be told by me rather than by letter. That was the coward's way out.

In case I did stop off at Crewe, I wrote reminding my mother I'd be delayed in coming home. I was going to see a girl I'd been in basic training with. And I wrote to Steve telling more lies, though at the time I didn't consider what I wrote as lies. Or not serious ones anyway. I wanted my bird in the hand and the one in the bush.

One day, while walking through the hospital grounds, I saw a bed of lupins not yet in flower and thought about Deirdre. I wondered if she had ever tracked down her lost husband. When I went back to the ward I wrote her a letter in which I told her I had written to her several times with the information I'd got from the post corporal. But just in case the letters hadn't reached her I was writing again. And in the belief that if you used the person's army number the letter would eventually reach them, I posted it. As with the previous letters I got no reply.

I came back to camp hoping for letters from Johnny. There weren't any. Nor did any come during the following weeks. But I was confident they would arrive. Maybe not before he sailed. But surely they would come.

* * *

Spring had arrived. The place of trees was a bouquet of forty shades of green new leaves. PT lessons were in full swing. I had two sessions in the morning and organized netball matches with other units in the vicinity. In between lessons, I went to the telephone exchange and the café. There one day I saw the sergeant

Sean had described. He was tall, handsome and arrogant-looking. Full of himself, as they'd say in Dublin. I found him attractive, and knew that before long I'd be dating him.

I felt happier than I had since before Dora died, even though everything was changing. So many of the handsome heroes were gone. Civilians now. Boyish-looking National Service men replaced them. And the rumour was gathering that the unit would be disbanded before the year was out.

Breda and Katy had their demobilization dates—Breda in the beginning of May, and Katy early in June. I pushed to the back of my mind the questions of how I'd exist without them, and when and where I'd be posted. Hoped for letters from Johnny. Tried to decide about Crewe and captivating the new sergeant.

* * *

One day in my storeroom, where I hadn't checked the equipment since the cold weather, I noticed that fourteen pairs of socks were missing. Maybe I'd put them on another shelf. I looked but they weren't there. I searched all the shelves. No sign of them. I was the only one with the key. Then I remembered Jock, a cheeky-faced girl from Glasgow. Urchin-like, good at PT and games. Once I suggested she'd be suitable for a course. She refused. 'I'd love doing it, Corp, but wouldna be any good out there in front.'

She had borrowed the key when we were snowed in. She wanted a skipping rope. 'But you can't skip in the snow,' I'd said.

'In the ablutions, not the snow,' she'd replied, looking at me as if I were daft. 'Concrete floors, bags of room between the lavs and sinks. I feel like an auld woman with getting no exercise,' she said with her head cocked to one side, reminding me of one of the Bisto Kids. I let her have the key. She returned it.

I thought no more about it until I missed the socks. Had she taken or misplaced them? They were knee-length, pure wool. They'd cost a lot to replace. But why would she want fourteen pairs of socks? I'd give her the benefit of the doubt for a while.

In the meantime I racked my brains trying to recall when they'd last been used. A hockey fixture before Christmas. After a game I'd wash and hang them to dry in the laundry room. I checked. No sign of them. I asked around. Had anyone seen them? Taken them by mistake? Bundled them in with their washing? Katy laughed at this question. 'Not notice twenty-eight hairy socks amongst your knickers? Jock nicked them, stands to reason.'

'Why would she do that?'

'Because she's a thief. Been nicking since she could walk, crawl or reach out her hand.'

'But what would she do with them?'

'Flog them.'

'Who'd want to buy long green-and-white hockey socks?'

'If the price is right you can flog anything. You'll have to charge her.'

'Oh God,' I exclaimed. It was the dread and fear of my life having to charge anyone, the only thing I disliked about having a rank. 'I don't think I could.'

'So how are you going to explain the next bare-legged hockey team? If you don't put Jock on a fizzer you'll be charged for the loss of WD property.'

'What if she denies taking them?'

'She probably will. Say I saw her with them. I'll be a witness.'

Breda was horrified at Katy's suggestion and delivered a lecture about false witness. Katy told her to belt up.

'I wasn't serious about giving evidence. But I am about letting Jock think I saw her with the socks. She's not as tough as she looks. In a gang on her home ground she might be. But not face to face with you. Talk to her. Make her feel sorry for you. She might still have them, and give them back to you.'

'And if she doesn't, or has already got rid of them, what then?'

'Charge her. See Miss Long. She'll arrange the hanging.'

* * *

'Jock, d'ye remember the day you wanted to skip and I lent you the key for the store room?'

'Aye,' she said, not meeting my eyes.

'Well, the thing is there were hockey socks in the stores and now I can't find them.'

Still not looking directly at me she asked, 'Got a fag?' I gave her one and a light.

'I was wondering if you moved them?'

173

Then, for the first time looking me in the eye, she swore she'd never seen them.

'I know someone who saw you with them. I'll have to charge you and she'll be a witness.'

'Your mate from Edinburgh?' she said derisively.

I ignored the remark and waited.

'OK,' she said. 'Give us another fag.'

I did and she grinned.

'I never thought to nick nothing when I went in. Then I saw the socks. I was broke. I knew blokes who'd buy them.'

'So you sold them?'

'Yeah, I flogged them—two bob a pair. Money for jam.'

'And thought you'd get away with it?'

'I never thought about it.'

Going against all I'd been taught about army discipline, I apologized.

'I'm sorry about having to charge you. If there was another way I wouldn't.'

'I don't care about charges. Been on dozens. Nothing to them. Silly lotta sods.'

She laughed. I tried not to but couldn't help smiling at her cheek. I gave her a few more fags then went to see Miss Long. Told her of the theft and Jock's admission and looked suitably abashed as she admonished me for my carelessness in lending the key.

'You'll be notified of the date and time of the charge,' she said when the lecture was finished. Jock served my meals as friendly and cocky as ever. Came to her PT lessons and cadged fags as if nothing out of the ordinary had happened.

* * *

On the following Monday at 8.45 a.m. I reported to the Sergeant-Major's office. I'd pressed my uniform the night before, polished my buttons and shoes to a high shine and wore my cap at the regulation army angle. Jock and another corporal were already in Miss Long's office, the corporal standing at ease, Jock to attention. I could see her uniform hadn't had a bang of an iron for many a day and her cap perched so far to the side of her head it was in danger of falling off. Miss Long and the corporal, with Jock between them and me behind, marched out of the office.

174

Miss Long gave the commands, halting us outside the CO's door where Jock's cap was removed and put on a chair. After knocking on the commander's door and being bidden to enter we marched in and halted before the desk. Miss Long read out the charge. Jock kept nudging me, trying to make me laugh. I gave my evidence. Then the CO questioned Jock. She answered in a broad Glaswegian dialect, one I'd never heard her use before, forcing the CO to halt the procedure and ask her to speak more clearly. Jock admitted the theft. 'But why?' asked the Commanding Officer. 'Didn't you realize it was stealing?'

'Didn't think, ma'am.'

Sentence was passed. 'Seven days confined to barracks. The cost of the socks deducted from your pay in weekly instalments.'

The trial was over. Miss Long about-turned us and marched us out. Jock retrieved her cap and put it on. On the way back to the billet I asked her why the cap had been removed.

'In case I threw it at the CO.'

'You wouldn't have?'

'Course I wouldn't. Blokes used to. Fix razor blades in them so they'd slash the face.'

'You're kidding.'

'Straight up. Specially blokes from the Gorbals.' She lit a fag. 'Seven days CB—that's nothing. Sometimes I don't leave the camp for fourteen.'

'But you'll miss the money.'

'Not too much. The army's fair. Only deducts small amounts.'

On two other occasions I was involved in charges when I was the prisoner in the dock. I committed the first offence on a damp misty morning walking back from a PT lesson at another camp. My hair was long overdue for a trim and straggled on my collar. I heard the sound of a car behind me and moved onto the grass verge to let it pass. Instead it slowed and stopped beside me. It was an army staff car which, driven by Forces personnel, ferried senior ranks, male and female, to their destinations. My first thought was that the passenger in the back seat had taken pity on me, as it had started to rain, and was about to offer me a lift. That idea fled the minute I saw the cross, creased, ancient face glaring at me above the lowered window, a woman of senior rank who reminded me of a vulture.

'Corporal,' she said in a voice used to being obeyed. 'Come here.'

I went close to the window, guessing I was in trouble.

'Your hair is a disgrace. Straggling down the back of your neck. What is the regulation length?'

'Two inches above the collar, ma'am.' Not a single hair showed beneath her cap. Baldy, I thought, as I stood to attention at an awkward angle on the grass verge. I gave at her demand my name, number, rank and unit. She ordered her driver to carry on. Looking after the car, I remembered Steve's contempt for the army's pettiness.

I was charged in due course and received an admonition, army parlance for a telling off. The other charge could have had serious consequences. But by the time it came about I was an old soldier and not above lying my way out of trouble.

I had applied for and been granted a seventy-two-hour pass, travel warrant and three days' ration money. I planned to go to London on Friday morning, meet a relation, have lunch and in the evening see a show.

I did all of these things. Walked down the Strand, thrilled at being in London. Feeling very sophisticated. Reflecting on the generosity of my cousin, who had treated me to lunch, the theatre and supper. Thinking about the Viennese steak I'd eaten, a flattened fried mince patty, but nevertheless quite tasty. And congratulating myself on how well the scam was working. In less than two hours I'd be back in camp. No problems getting in unnoticed. By the time I arrived the duty corporal would have done her rounds. My empty bed was accounted for as, according to her list, I was in London. Saturdays and Sundays few checks were made. I'd sleep late. Breakfast in the café on my ill-gotten gains. Go for a walk. Back to the café for coffee. Maybe see the sergeant Sean had said he'd introduce me to. We'd clicked without Sean's help, and had a loose arrangement to have lunch in Woking one day. Saturday might be the day. And on Sundays I had a standing invitation to Betty's.

I began to cross Waterloo Bridge, stopped to look at the river and thought about Vivienne Leigh and Robert Taylor. Only one thing marred my pleasure. I was wearing the horrible uniform. Forced to because my lovely tweed coat hadn't been cleaned since I joined up. The coat smelled of me and all the girls who'd borrowed it. The cleaners in Camberley had promised it for Thursday—it wasn't ready.

After gazing at the river for a while I walked on to the station. Crowds milled around, mostly army personnel. I was no sooner in the doors thatn two military policewomen pounced—the enemies of all other ranks, always on the lookout for the most trivial breaches of army regulations. They had spotted my fully fashioned non-issue stockings. Another admonition, I thought, 'Ça ne fait rien,' a French phrase very popular with the troops, the equivalent, so I believed, of 'I couldn't care less'.

The MPs didn't mention stockings, but asked what I was doing in London. God directed me, as my mother would have said, and I replied, 'I'm here for the weekend. Meeting someone here later on in the station.'

They asked to see my pass. I showed it. 'And your AB64 Part Two.' Which should have been in my left breast pocket but wasn't. In my mind's eye I saw it on my bed where I'd left it while I had pressed my tunic. I was in serious trouble. No proof of identity. I could be a deserter. There were thousands of deserters in the country. The pass could have been stolen or found.

Passing soldiers slagged the two Red Caps, women who towered over me. Tall as American basketball players.

'Pick on someone your own size, Lofty.'

'I could fancy you on a dark night.'

'A pitch-dark night.'

These were the gist of the remarks as between the giants I was marched to the Railway Transport Officers' room, from where my unit was telephoned and confirmation given that I was who I said I was. Not a deserter and in London on a seventy-two-hour pass. Panic assailed me. I'd be let go. But unless it was soon I'd miss the last train back to camp and be forced to find a lodging. There was the waiting room. I could doss there. But I didn't fancy the idea. The RTO chivvied the MPs. The office was crowded with military personnel wanting train times to the north, south, east and west.

'Better get a move on, her train goes in five minutes.'

'But I'm not catching a train. I'm on a weekend pass.'

'Not anymore you're not. You've been ordered back to your unit.'

The one who spoke had a smug expression in her eyes. 'We've put paid to that,' it conveyed. Her colleague reminded me of the heinous crime I'd committed. Out without my identity book. Inwardly I sighed with relief. I was going back to camp, which had been my intention all along.

They marched me to the waiting train. Running the gauntlet of sneering, jeering soldiers who mocked their lack of femininity, though they were careful not to overstep the mark. Women in the military police were empowered to arrest men.

They stood guard each side of the carriage door. I lolled back in my seat preening my feathers, knowing that compared to my warders I was a raving beauty.

* * *

The following Monday I was charged.

The CO, a pleasant middle-aged woman, lectured me on the gravity of leaving camp without any proof of identity. 'I have always judged you as a responsible person. One who could go far in the army.'

I looked suitably abashed.

'You do realize that for such an offence you could be reduced to the ranks.'

'Yes, ma'am.' Oh God, I'd lose my stripes. Revert to being a part-time instructor. My pay reduced. The allowance to my mother back to half a crown a week. That would make for happy homecomings. These thoughts went through my mind while the CO considered what my sentence should be.

She spoke. 'However, as your weekend in London was ruined I've decided to be lenient. I think you've had sufficient punishment, learned a lesson, and will never again leave camp without proof of your identity.'

'No ma'am.' My relief was overwhelming. The tears I'd held back fell. I wanted to thank her profusely. Apologize. Make promises. Not allowed.

'Charge dismissed.' I could have gone round the desk and kissed her. Not allowed. Might be construed by the Sergeant-Major as an attempted assault, certainly as conduct not befitting an NCO.

She deserved a salute but without my cap that wasn't possible. So I settled for, 'Thank you, ma'am.'

TWENTY

The handsome, arrogant sergeant's name was Mike. He came from a mining village in Derbyshire. He had won a scholarship to the grammar school and hoped this was his way of escape from the pit. He hated the mine, its wheel dominating the village, the never-ending battle his mother waged against the dirt. His black-faced father with blue-scarred forehead. Grammar school could take him away from all of it. Take him into college, or even, if he was lucky, university. Other miners' sons had achieved it. But when he was fourteen his father told him he had to find work. Keeping four children was beyond his means. He could go down the pit or join the army as a boy soldier. He cried and his mother cried for his lost chance. He chose the army and never regretted his choice.

I listened, not particularly interested, or so I thought at the time. For almost everyone I'd known had had to earn their keep from the time they were fourteen.

I found him humourless. Never once did he make me laugh. I compared him unfavourably to Steve and Johnny. Unlike them he didn't stroll along the banks of the canal with an arm round my waist stopping now and then to admire a flower or a bird in flight, or kiss me lingeringly.

He almost marched along the tow path, erect as if on the parade ground. And even off duty he carried his swagger stick tucked underneath his arm. But what I disliked most about him was how he kissed me. Through his closed thin lips I felt the pressure of his teeth. They hurt my mouth.

One night my lips were swollen and Katy remarked on them. 'Watch him and don't lead him on. Blokes like him are dangerous.'

'How d'ye mean dangerous?' asked Breda.

'In the way I explained to you when you told me about the dance in the Canadian mess.'

'Honest to God?'

'Honest to whoever you like.'

'I thought he was gorgeous. And he's a good Catholic. Never misses mass. Still, I suppose you could be right. My Bob's not a bit like that. He's a dote. A lamb.'

She enlarged some more on Bob's qualities and how things were getting serious between them. Katy adroitly changed the subject by asking me why I didn't pack Mike in.

'All you do is moan about him. I think he's a right pain in the arse. Fancy him noticing that the velvet collar on your coat was shabby and making you take off your coat before he brought you into the sergeant's mess.'

'You're right. I should pack him in. The trouble is there's so few decent-looking fellas left. And I like having someone to take me out.'

'Don't we know it,' Katy laughed. I knew she was right, I should finish with Mike. I nearly had a week ago. We were babysitting for Betty. She'd left a pie baking for our supper and when Mike took it out he commented that the oven was filthy. I was astounded that a man would notice such a thing. In Ireland, where immaculate ovens weren't high on the list of housekeeping priorities, he'd have been regarded as moff, or a blood oul' Mary Ann who should be wearing a diddy bib. But what incensed me was that he should criticize Betty, who showered us with hospitality.

How ill-mannered he is, I thought, watching him wolf the pie, but postponed chucking him over for another time, using the excuse that I couldn't risk a quarrel while Mary was in bed. But when he switched on the radio to hear the Palm Court Orchestra play romantic music and asked me to sit by him on the sofa I made an excuse not to. Tonight there'd be no clashing of teeth. I pretended to have a headache, left as soon as Betty and Sean returned, and offered my cheek for a kiss when we arrived at the billets.

* * *

Breda took Bob home and the family took him to their hearts.

'So,' asked Katy, 'when is the wedding?'

'We'll have to get jobs first, then decide and start saving.'

'What'll you try for?'

'Telephonist, I suppose. And you?'

I shrugged. 'Get married to the right bloke. Johnny, if I was to hear from him.'

'But what about Steve? What about Crewe and the engagement.'

'Oh God, I don't know. I seldom give him a thought. Johnny's always in my mind. I could be happy with him forever and ever. And marriage is forever and ever.'

'That's you all over. Steve's panting for you. Johnny's never written. Unavailable, so he's the one you want. Think you want. You don't love either of them. You're in love with love.'

'You're a right know-all, Katy. How d'ye know what goes on in my mind?'

'Because I've listened to you blethering on for years. Steve or Johnny. Johnny or Steve. And at the same time you're risking having your teeth put down your throat every night.'

It was good-natured bantering but Breda found it necessary to defend me.

'I was lucky I only ever fell for Bob. But marriage is serious so you have to be sure if it's really someone you love. Supposing you finished with Johnny and Steve and started over again? But maybe you wouldn't find anyone else. It'd be terrible to finish up an old maid. A woman has to get a husband. There's nothing else for her.'

I lied and said, 'I wouldn't care. I'd sign on. In any case I've bags of time before I finish this engagement. Two years in June. June 1950. What will you go for, Katy, when you're demobbed?'

'Nursing.'

'Nursing, I couldn't stand the sight of blood,' said Breda. 'I'd rather scrub floors than bandage a cut. I nearly faint when I see blood.'

The conversation had depressed me. I didn't want to think of a time when they'd both be gone. When the unit was disbanded. When I'd be on the move to God only knew where. Why did things have to change? I might never see Katy or Breda again. We'd promise to write and would for a while. Then one or the other wouldn't answer a letter. Like Johnny. We'd promise to write and wouldn't. I'd lose touch with all those I loved. The only solution was never to get involved. That way you were protected. Never suffer the pain of separation. But I couldn't live like that. I needed people. If I'd been a loner I'd never have known Katy, Breda, Sylvia, Sean and Betty, Johnny, Steve. The girls in basic training. Always I'd have to risk the pain of losing those I loved. Suffer when they left. For all the joy and love they'd given me the parting had to be endured.

* * *

Tonight was the night I would finish with Mike. We'd been invited to a birthday party. He had told me to wear a particular dress. It was one I liked but resented being ordered to wear it. 'I want to feel proud of you,' he'd said when I protested.

He was waiting for me where we usually met. At first I didn't recognize him in civilian suit. Navy blue rough serge. Badly cut. Tight across his chest, the sleeves too short. I hadn't spent four years handling good cloth and tailoring not to spot rubbish when I saw it. He wore a white shirt and a hard-boiled collar, reminding me of a culchie up in Dublin for the day.

Yet there he stood preening like a peacock. Then I remembered his rearing and felt so sorry for him I decided I'd leave chucking him until our next date.

Which was at a dance in the gymnasium. I wore a pale lemon jersey dress. The one he liked. He was late turning up. In the meantime I danced with other men who bought me drinks. Mostly lemonade. While dancing a foxtrot, Mike cut in.

'I've been watching you,' he said. 'Spreading yourself around,' and he held me closer than was comfortable. He's jealous, I thought, and was flattered. He bought me a drink. Neat gin. I'd developed a liking for neat gin when the buyer could afford it. We danced again. Then I had two more gins. I loved the taste, the smell, and its effect on me. I felt light and floaty and languorous so that I leant into him. Halfway through a waltz he suggested we go out for a breath of fresh air.

We found a place from where we couldn't be seen yet near enough to hear the band's romantic music. The April night was warm, the sky full of stars. I wanted kissing and caressing and wasn't aware of the pressure of his teeth on my lips, anaesthetized as they were by the effects of raw gin. But then his hand slipped to my bottom and began circling it and his knee was attempting to force itself between my legs. Alarm bells rang. Katy's warning flashed through my mind. I pushed him away. He went berserk. 'You little bitch,' he hissed. 'You led me on,' his voice was raised. Then he lowered it and whispered, 'Please, I won't hurt you. I won't make you pregnant. I'll use something, honest to God.'

I moved farther from him. He grabbed me by the shoulders, bent close to my face. 'D'ye know what you're doing to me? You've got me on the verge of a breakdown. You'll be the cause of me needing psychiatric treatment.'

I pushed him away and ran towards the billet, terrified that at any minute his hand would descend on my shoulder, another part of my mind thinking, Well that's the first time anyone's tried moral blackmail and him a good Catholic. From the gymnasium I could hear the band playing 'This Is the Story of a Starry Night'. The tune embedded itself in my brain. I seldom hear the song now but when I do I remember that night.

* * *

I didn't book a sleeper on the mail train. It wasn't worth it to Crewe. I'd had a letter two days previously from Steve confirming our arrangements. His train from Glasgow would arrive an hour before mine. He'd be waiting for me on the platform. He had booked accommodation for us. He was counting the minutes. Found it hard to believe that in such a short time we'd be together again.

Katy had lent me her Shetland sweater. I wore it over a green and cream plaid straight skirt and round my neck the silver locket. Betty had restyled my hair. With my ration money I'd splashed out on a pink lipstick and matching nail polish. 'Take this,' Betty said before I left, handing me a small phial of Houbigant scent. 'That'll turn his head,' she smiled and wished me luck.

On my way to Waterloo and the tube to Euston I recalled the first time I'd seen Steve. Love at first sight. Eyes the colour of a young kitten's. I trembled inside at the thought of seeing him again. How could I have ever doubted my love for him? I adored him. This time tomorrow we'd be engaged. Soon after married. His wife forever and ever.

I'd brought a book by A.J. Cronin and a magazine. Once on

183

the mail train I opened the novel and pretended to be engrossed in it. Not that I minded talking to a fellow passenger; it depended on who it was. On the Irish Mail you could be landed with one who talked non-stop, sometimes the worse for drink. So until I'd sussed them out I pretended to read. In reality I was thinking about Steve and our reunion. How he'd embrace me, kiss me, tell me he loved me.

The carriage was filling up. A nun sat next to me. Then a young woman with a baby and expecting another one. An old woman dressed in black joined us.

The opposite seat was empty. Once the train started I'd move to it. Take off my shoes and stretch out unless the baby fell asleep first and the mother laid him down. But just as the train began to move, four men came aboard. Irishmen, already three sheets to the wind. Two of them carried a crate of stout.

The old and young woman got into talk. 'God bless the child, how old is he?'

'It's a girl. She's eight months.'

'By the time she's twelve month old she'll have a head of hair. My own were the same. Bald for months. Everyone thinking they were boys. Were you over on a visit?'

'I wasn't, I've been living over this two years in a place called Islington. I'm going home. My mother's had a bad stroke. Lost the use of herself and can't speak a word.'

'The crathur. I've just buried my brother with the same complaint. Never sick a day in his life. A fine man, Lord have mercy on him. In the whole of his health and then downed like a slaughtered ox. You never know from one minute to the next. It's God's will.'

''Tis so. Was there no one to come with you?'

'Not a one. Not that many a one wasn't willing but couldn't lay their hands on the fare.' Despite myself I listened to the conversation. ''Twas the same with me. My neighbour would willingly have come but hadn't a farthing,' the young woman said.

The nun laid down a devotional book she'd been reading. 'I couldn't help overhearing. I'm sorry for your troubles and I'll pray for your mother and your brother's soul.'

I made overtures to the baby and in no time was one of the four. We told each other where we came from at home. The other women were from the west of Ireland. Another long journey lay ahead after they reached Dublin.

They discovered an acquaintance in common and talked about the coincidence. The ease with which we spoke to each other. The same thing happened on English trains but only between troops. On a journey with civilians there was no social intercourse.

Travelling to and from Brighton and on my way to the hospital in Surrey not a word was exchanged. All of a sudden I longed to be in Ireland, where on bus, train or tram, or walking down a street, someone would pass the time of day.

The old woman and the exhausted grieving young mother fell asleep, the nun returned to her book, and I to my thoughts of Steve.

Between Watford Junction and Rugby I felt the expectant excitement begin to ebb, doubts and anxiety taking its place.

Fear gripped me. What would become of me if Steve wasn't at Crewe? Supposing he had missed his connections. Had been taken ill suddenly. If only I could have telephoned before I'd left the camp to get his assurance that all was going according to plan. But only in a matter of life and death could a telephone call be made from the camp. Otherwise it was the public call-box. Outside the camp. Frequently out of action and always a queue, besides needing a sackful of coins.

The men finished the crate of drink and brought in another from the corridor. They drank and smoked Woodbines and Player's Navy Cut. Coughed and hawked. The women woke. The men offered drinks and thick sandwiches from newspaper wrapping. The drink was declined but the old and young woman accepted the sandwiches. The baby chewed on a crust.

The train sped on through the night and another set of fears assailed my mind. Where were Steve and I going to stay? Had he booked a double room? In the middle of the night, thrilled by seeing him, I might be carried away and agree. Fear would play a part. If I refused, where could I go in the middle of the night? And if we were pretending to be a married couple I'd die of embarrassment, the lies, the looks, the sniggering.

And supposing he made me pregnant. And afterwards I heard from Johnny. Realized he was the one I really loved. That his fear was about his religion—not black babies. The heat in the train had been turned up. The vent was behind my legs. They were roasting. Sweat poured off me. The carriage stank of drink and tobacco. The locket was strangling me. I undid it and put it in my handbag. And I wished I was going straight on to Dublin. By the time the line began branching I'd made my decision. I was going straight to Dublin. I convinced myself that Steve wouldn't be at Crewe. But in case he was, I hid in the lavatory. The train stayed for a long time in Crewe taking on mail. He might come looking in case I had fallen asleep. Twice while I was hiding a guard banged on the door and shouted. 'The toilet's not to be used while the train is stationary.'

I shouted back that I wasn't using it. I was making up and doing my hair.

We were on our way again. But I stayed inside the stinking cell until, through the muffled glass, I saw the lights disappear. Then I used the lavatory, splashed my face with cold water and went back to my carriage. At that moment I felt neither guilt nor pity, only an enormous sense of relief that I'd had a narrow escape. I slept until the train arrived at Holyhead.

On the crossing I did dwell on what I'd done. On Steve being there on the platform waiting for me. His disappointment. Worrying that something had happened to me. Enquiring if there was another boat train coming up from Euston. Then dejectedly walking through the night to wherever he had booked for us to stay. But once I was on the train into Dublin I had again convinced myself I'd done the right thing.

There was no one to meet me. I took a cab home. My mother always hated being taken unawares and berated me for arriving unexpectedly. 'I'm only half-dressed. I was pulling up my knickers when you knocked. And the fire's not lit.' I followed her into the kitchen where she soon recovered her good humour, put the kettle on, then knelt to light the fire. Fixed an old tray and sheet of newspaper in front of it. As usual, once a blaze started the sheet of paper caught fire, and, as usual, with her strong square hands my mother squeezed the life from it.

'I thought,' she said, as she began making breakfast, 'you were stopping off to see a friend.'

'Her granny took a stroke and died, so I couldn't. The place is looking grand.'

'Sure I don't know myself with the comfort, with the money that's rolling in. Your poor Daddy, if only he was here to share it.' She shed a few tears, then went to the bottom of the stairs to call my sister for work. Even with her hair tossed and the sleep still in her eyes she looked pretty.

On the mantelpiece there was a photograph of my brother in his RAF uniform.

'He never sent *me* one,' I complained.

'He might,' my mother retorted, 'if you ever answered his letters.'

I told her of the girl dying with meningitis. She said, 'The Lord have mercy on the little girl,' and mentioned a dozen deaths of young and old in the neighbourhood. She seldom listened to what you had to say, her mind always occupied with what she had to say next. Unless I was to confide in her about blokes. She'd revel in my indecision over Johnny and Steve. Advise me. Recall similar episodes in her single days. Be intrigued as to what was Johnny's fear that he couldn't tell me. Jump to the conclusion that he was married. I told her very little about boyfriends. For when her humour was bad or we rowed she would throw the confidences in my face. Criticize men she had never seen. Tell me they were after my money—the forty pounds I'd get when I finished my extra two years. And warn me of all the diseases I could catch gum-sucking Billy and Jack. And as for meeting a man in the middle of the night at a railway station, had she been the sort of Catholic to bring the priest on you, he'd have been in the kitchen before you could say Jack Robinson.

This time I had plenty to tell her that would hold her interest. The Brighton and Horsham saga. We were still talking about it after my sister had left for work. Several pots of tea were made and drunk as she demanded a blow-by-blow description of what they looked like. Did they resemble my father, talk like him, about him? Ask about her, my brother and sister? Enquire how she managed for money? Did they admire me? Ask me to visit them again? Would I say they had money?

When there were no more questions to be asked for the time being she summed them up. A pair of mean, miserable bastards who'd never have an hour's luck for treating an orphaned child as they had. 'Sure you wouldn't treat a poor oul' stray dog like that. But one thing's sure and certain, she didn't suck your granny's blood. Your granny was Irish and it was after her your father took. God love you, you must have got an awful drop when you realized what they were like. To think of my child being treated like that. The curse of God on the pair of them. A lodging-house-keeper, that's what she is. That'd account for the big house and Brighton being a seaside place. And lodging-house-keepers are renowned for their niggardliness.'

During the first few days at home I visited relations and had lunch in town with one. In Robert Roberts, a step up in the world after the village café and the NAFFI. Strong, sweet, hot coffee and a selection of delicious cream cakes to follow crisp golden chips and a steak. Beef steak, not whale or shark meat. I saw a couple of films alone. Went to the skating rink once and that was an end to my outings. Skating without a partner was an embarrassment, dancing alone unheard of. Standing without the company of another girl pretending to be engrossed in con-versation when in reality each of you was watching and hoping that a fella would cross the divide and ask you up, you'd feel like a leper. I'd lost touch with the girls I once went to dances with. So no dancing.

I spent nights alone listening to Radio Athlone, more often than not learning about the state of farming in Ireland. Waiting for my mother to come home from her active social life and my sister from the crowd of fellas and girls she went about with. Gazing into the fire, bored and lonely, I regretted ditching Steve. We'd have been engaged, and, said a voice in my head, 'lost your virginity and already pregnant'. All the same I hedged my bets and wrote a long, long letter filled with lies. How I had fainted at Euston, broke my heart crying when I came around realizing I'd missed the train to Crewe, begged the stationmas-ter to send a message to Crewe saying I'd be up on the morning train. How he was the surliest man I'd ever met and refused.

I begged Steve to write to me in Dublin. I could meet him on the way back. I told him how much I loved and missed him and posted the letter. He never replied. As the days passed and no reply came I was consumed with guilt. He was too hurt by what I had done. Devastated, I kept picturing him. His gorgeous blue eyes. I'd kiss his photograph a dozen times as tears blinded me. But as days passed and no letter came I changed my tune. Convincing myself that he had never come to Crewe. He too had got cold feet at the last minute. There was a pair of us in it. And I consoled myself with thoughts of Johnny. There'd be a letter waiting for me at camp. Maybe several. All arrived togeth-er. In fact, when I returned there was only one letter waiting for me. From Bubbles, now living in San Diego and expecting her first baby. I never heard from either Johnny or Steve again.

Breda invited everyone she knew even slightly to her demob party. Even the spiv who'd offered her a roll of oilcloth for a feel of her knee. Had she known what a lesbian was, and that two of her guests were practising ones, she might have drawn the line there. I had suspected there was something out of the ordinary about these girls. They were mannish-looking, never dated, wore trousers whenever possible, drank pints and were expert dart players. Women that in Dublin would have been described as being 'a lump of a Jack'.

Before I joined up a scandal broke in Dublin about two homosexuals. I remember the jokes that went the rounds. 'A man fell off a buoy in Howth and cockle-pickers in Merrion were demanding danger money.' From the sniggers I knew there was something dirty about that. But couldn't even hazard a guess as to what. And when I was in basic training it was stressed that no girl should lie on another's bed or sleep with a girl. Edith explained that there were men who'd do a frog if it stopped hopping. And according to her Dad there were women also that way inclined.

That was the extent of my knowledge until the night I saw the two mannish-looking girls kissing passionately. I was so shocked I woke Katy to tell her.

'It's the middle of the night,' she said, exaggerating the time. 'Couldn't it have waited till morning?' She sat up and lit a cigarette.

'It's just that I was so shocked.' And I told her what I'd seen.

'They're lesbians.'

'What's that?'

'Sometimes you're as thick as Breda.' Then she gave me a graphic description of how lesbians satisfied their sexual urges.

'That's disgusting. I've never heard anything like it in my life.'

She stubbed out her cigarette. And turning her back on me said, 'Well, you have now. And don't panic, they go for their own kind. You're safer with them than a hell of a lot of men.'

A little later I went to the ablutions. One of the lesbians was there. Like me in her pyjamas, carrying her sponge bag. 'OK, Pad?' she asked. She didn't have horns, she was her usual friendly self. Katy, as usual, was right.

The night of the party we dressed in our best. Katy looked glowing, gorgeous. She needed little make-up, and what she did use was applied quickly and with expertise. Vanishing-cream, face powder, a little touch of pencil to her well-defined, arched eyebrows. A last touch of powder on her high cheekbones and tip-tilted nose, and then her tangee lipstick. She put on her white Burberry, turned its collar up and tied, not buckled, the belt. Katy had style.

Some had lifts to the pub. Others, including Breda, Bob, me, Katy and Sylvia, choose to walk. Bob and Breda walked in front with linked arms. From behind we good-naturedly and loudly joked about 'Love's Young Dream'.

We crossed the bridge over the canal. I lagged behind, leaning over it looking down at the towpath along which I had so often strolled with Johnny. Wishing he was with me. Wondering why he had never answered my many letters. Wondering was he in Palestine and not Egypt. Had he been killed there. Was that the reason I had never heard.

'Will you hurry up,' Katy shouted back. 'We won't get seats if you don't.'

I caught them up. We climbed the hill, down to the other side and proceeded. 'Ginger has laid on the duty truck to take us back if it's not called out for something official. And if it is he reminded me we're not to miss the last bus.' I added what he had also said—that in the state we'd be in we'd finish up in the canal.

'He'll tell us again in the pub. Nag, nag, nag,' said Katy.

'He's like a mother hen,' Sylvia added. And Katy laughed, 'How we get back is the least of our worries.'

The public house was called the Rose and Crown. It was hundreds of years old, with tables and benches of rough-hewn oak. In one corner sat a group of old men playing 'shove ha'penny'. A few regulars stood at the bar. We knew them all and on demob party night soldiers bought the old men drinks.

At each table the men set out kitties, laid down their cigarettes and matches. Everyone relaxed, happy, looking forward to a great night. Despite the kitty, drinks were already being sent to our table for Breda. She was well liked and this was the men's way of toasting her and wishing her well.

All she drank was lemonade. Most of the girls ordered cider. It was cheaper and tasted pleasanter than beer. Breda told me she had invited Mike but he couldn't make it.

'Thanks be to God,' I said to myself.

Despite her protests, drinks continued to arrive for Breda. Anything intoxicating she passed on to Katy, Sylvia and me. Within no time we were drunk without realizing it. From time to time she became tearful at the thought of leaving us the following day. Bob gave her a hanky and told her to cheer up. 'You've got a good time coming, kid.'

'I know,' she snuffled and smiled, 'only I'll miss you all so much. I'll be sorry to go, but shed no tears. Two weeks and I'll be a free woman. Sorry to leave you lot but not the soddin' army. No more saluting po-faced officers. Yes ma'am, no ma'am, three bags full ma'am. Bully beef and brown blankets. All the bull.'

'Roll on June,' Katy crowed.

Packets of crisps were passed round. We fished out the little blue twists of paper and salted them, shaking the bag to distribute it. And guzzled the cider to slake our thirst.

Sean, Betty, Ginger and some of the older policemen sat at the next table. Younger men came to ours. Offering more crisps, cigarettes, chatting us up. Hoping for someone to walk back with, snog with. There were no takers.

Someone started to sing. Soon we were all singing the corny favourites. 'Kelliher's Jam', 'Coming Round the Mountain When She Comes', 'Take Me Back to Dear Old Blighty', and 'Bless 'em All'. The younger girls raised their voices to compete, singing the latest popular songs, but didn't stand a chance. Vera Lynn's romantic and melancholy songs had an airing.

We smoked and drank, sang and laughed, by this time at anything. We were having a smashing party. Sean and Betty left. Ginger got word that the duty truck had been called out and reminded us before he left not to miss the last bus.

Courting couples began to leave, including the two lesbians. The kitty was spent, the table filled with drinks. Katy, Sylvia and the soldiers did their best to empty the glasses before time was called. Managed to empty many of them before the landlord called 'time gentlemen please'.

Breda urged us to hurry or we'd miss the last bus. 'We'll walk,' said Katy, hardly able to stand, and she staggered from table to table, making for the lavatory. A fellow Scotsman told her of the 'sair' head she'd have in the morning. 'Sod off,' she replied and collapsed onto his lap.

With Sylvia's help she made it to the lavatory, still ranting about wanting to walk. We humoured her while Breda bundled her into the white Burberry and, with Bob's help, got her outside. The bus was approaching and Katy still protesting that she wanted to walk back to camp. She swayed and would have fallen except for the hold Bob and Breda had on her. They humoured her, promising that if she got on, they'd let her off halfway back to walk the rest of the way. 'Promise,' said Katy, and Breda promised.

The bus stopped. There was a rush to board. The conductor shouted, 'Standing-room only.' Soldiers and girls pushed and shoved, sang and giggled. 'Move along. Move along,' urged the conductor. Bob got separated from Breda, who still held on to Katy's arm. I held the other one. The aisle was full; now there was only room on the platform. Sylvia sat halfway up the stairs, ignoring the conductor's warning that she was blocking the stairway. I caught hold of the silvery pole joining platform to ceiling. Katy protested that she didn't want to link me and Breda, wrenched herself free and clung also to the pole. Behind us soldiers jostled, swore and sang obscene versions of army songs. The conductor pressed the bell and the bus moved off. The soldiers began to quarrel. The conductor pressed through the crowded aisle shouting, 'Fares please, any more fares.'

Then for a moment the singing, swearing soldiers were silent. Breda took advantage of the lull and with her eyes full of tears sang to me and Katy, 'I'll be seeing you in all the old familiar places.' The row started again amongst the soldiers. Down the hill drove the bus. Katy's eyes were closing, she was falling asleep on her feet. The argument became heated. One soldier pushed another. They fell against us at the same moment as the bus suddenly braked and Katy was gone. I was still holding tightly to the pole where her hand had been clamped above or below mine. It wasn't there anymore. A voice screamed, then another. Mine and Breda's. 'Jesus Christ,' a man exclaimed. I stood transfixed, as if the pole had pierced and pinned me to the platform.

People pushed past me, jumped into the road. Someone said, 'I think it was a horse. Came out of a field.' Then I screamed again and again, 'Katy, Katy, oh Katy,' before getting off the bus. I saw the horse. It was white and I thought it was a horse, only a white horse. Then I saw the other white figure and ran to it. Breda got there first and knelt beside Katy. Lifting her shoulders, cradling her against her breast, blood pouring from her head.

Someone shouted, 'Get an ambulance.' I saw the driver and conductor kneeling close by, and heard the voice saying and repeating, 'I was trying not to hit the horse, that's what I was trying to do.' Breda was praying, saying an Act of Contrition. I stroked Katy's hand and watched the blood stain her white Burberry, thinking that her lovely coat would be ruined. And calling her name. Pleading, 'Katy, Katy, don't die. Katy, sure you won't die Katy, please.'

The ambulance and police came. The police ordered everyone back on the bus. An ambulance man took Katy from Breda's arms. Then she was on a stretcher being carried to the ambulance. Breda and I begged to be allowed go with her. Breda, who couldn't stand the sight of blood, was saturated in Katy's. Sylvia pulled rank, such as it was, insisting she had the right to accompany Katy. But we were all ordered by the police to board the bus. After the ambulance left, they came in to question us until, realizing that everyone with the exception of Breda was drunk, they abandoned the attempt. After enquiring, 'Are you OK, mate?' the driver was told to take the bus to its destination, and for the journey back to camp a constable remained with the conductor, questioning him and taking notes.

After stripping off our blood-stained clothes, Breda and I, ignoring King's Regulations, lay on my bed, arms round each other, and cried ourselves to sleep. During the night we woke, showered, and went to our own beds, where we lay until morning crying quietly, wondering how soon we'd hear news of Katy. Towards the morning we slept. And woke when it was light.

For a moment I didn't remember the previous night. Then I saw the empty bed: the box of face powder, the spare packet of cigarettes. And, hanging on her locker door, her tunic, buttoned, carefully hung. Katy was a smart girl.

'D'ye think she's dead?' Breda whispered. We both started crying again.

I wished I was at home. Sitting before the fire. Sitting with my mother. Her endless questions making me face the reality of what had happened. Which I hadn't yet, for every second I expected to hear Katy's annoyed voice asking, 'What are you two doing awake at this time. And why are the two of you greetin'?' Then reaching for her fags. In between questions my mother would be asking God to spare Katy if it was his will. Then turning on me. 'If the lotta you hadn't been mouldy drunk it wouldn't have happened.' Giving me the opportunity to release my anger. Shout at her. Tell her she had no feelings. Didn't understand what I was going through. She'd make me hot sweet tea. Order me to drink it. Oh God, how I longed to be at home instead of in a curtainless, comfortless, barrack room. A room where girls were sleeping, snoring, dreaming. A room that was as it always was at this time in the morning except for Katy's empty bed.

'When d'ye think we'll get any news?' Breda whispered again.

'When company office opens. Miss Long is bound to ring the hospital.'

Girls woke up and began the usual morning rush to get ready for breakfast and work until they remembered and the atmosphere became hushed. They moved slowly, spoke more quietly, many cried openly. Others came to Breda and me asking for news.

Sylvia arrived, her eyes red and puffy.

'I wonder what'll happen about your demob, Breda?'

'I expect they'll postpone it. I couldn't face anything like that today.'

'The two of you look terrible. Did you get any sleep?'

'Not much,' I said. 'I still think I had a nightmare. It doesn't seem real. I'd love a cup of tea, but I couldn't go to the cook-house.'

'I'll bring two mugs. I won't be long.'

Before Sylvia returned, the Company Sergeant-Major arrived. Katy was still alive. Her head injuries were serious and she had been moved to a hospital in Oxford.

Miss Long cancelled PT lessons for the day and detailed me to accompany Breda to the MI room to be checked for delayed shock. 'Your demobilization will be postponed. The MO will verify that you're not fit to travel.' Then, addressing the remainder of the girls, she told them, 'I'll keep you informed as I get news from the hospital. It is a terrible tragedy, but we must carry on as usual. You will all report for work.'

There followed a time filled with a terrible sense of loss. Sometimes I fooled myself that Katy was on leave, on a course, even posted to another camp where very soon I'd visit her. But the pretence was difficult to sustain. And then I'd again relive the dreadful night, when one minute Katy's hand was above or below mine on the pole and the next it wasn't. And I'd upbraid myself for not taking better care of her. Telling myself, if only we'd walked home. It wasn't that far. She might have stumbled or fallen. Even into the canal. But that wasn't deep, we could have pulled her out.

Only through Miss Long did we hear news of Katy. She was still unconscious, despite surgery. Once I queued for ages at a public phone box and got through to the hospital. I lied, saying I was a relative. Waited and waited for a connection to Katy's ward, feeding coins into the box as the pips demanded them until the supply ran out.

* * *

The weeks passed and Katy was still in a coma. For hours, almost a whole day, sometimes I'd forget this. And then back the realization would come. My friend, someone I loved so much, who had enjoyed life so much, was in a hospital ward, unaware of her surroundings. Being washed and fed, turned over, creamed and powdered. How she'd loathe that.

My anguish would have been easier to bear if I'd had Breda to talk to. But Breda was now a civilian living with her parents in Southampton and working as a receptionist. And Sean and Betty had been posted to Otterburn. There was only Sylvia left. She was sometimes willing to relive the night and speculate as to whether or not Katy would recover consciousness and if she did whether she would be brain-damaged. But more often than not she advised me to try to put the tragedy out of my mind.

I began to wish that Katy would die and said this to Sylvia, who was horrified.

'That's no way to think. At any moment she could come round. Make a full recovery.'

'But supposing she doesn't?'

'You must never lose hope.'

We both did when news came that Katy had suffered severe brain damage and would be in a vegetative state for the rest of her life. From then on I prayed fervently, though not sure if I believed any longer in the God I was praying to, that she would die, that if Heaven did exist she'd be there and if it didn't, extinct.

I should have gone to see her. Touched her, held her hand, kissed her cheek.

I convinced myself that the reason I didn't was because there was no one to come with me. Sylvia said she also would like to visit Katy but was now working every weekend preparing for when the unit disbanded. But in our hearts we knew neither of us would have gone to Oxford. For neither of us had the courage to look on Katy as she was. Three months after the accident Katy died. Her funeral coincided with the day I was leaving for my new camp. Sylvia went in my place, along with an ATS subaltern and the Company Sergeant-Major as representatives of the unit.

I bid Sylvia good-bye, kissed and hugged her. Remembered our good times, her good-naturedness, her tall stories. Knowing it was unlikely I'd ever see her again. I said good-bye to the camp. To the cricket pavilion, the place of the trees. To Betty and Sean's house, now occupied by another family who'd come with an advance party of the new unit.

I'd miss them all. I'd never forget them. Not Johnny nor Steve. I'd remember them all. And the place where for nearly two years I believed I had found Tír na nÓg.